D1302789

It's Our Serve!

Smashing Recipes from
The Junior League
of
Long Island

Illustrations by Polly Keener

For additional copies of IT'S OUR SERVE!
use the coupons at the back of the book or contact:

JLLI Publications
The Junior League of Long Island, Inc.
1395 Old Northern Boulevard
Roslyn, New York 11576
(516) 484-0649

COPYRIGHT © 1989 BY JUNIOR LEAGUE OF LONG ISLAND, INC.
ROSLYN, NEW YORK
ALL RIGHTS RESERVED
FIRST EDITION
First Printing: 10,000 copies, May 1989

ISBN 0-9621722-0-0

Dedication

IT'S OUR SERVE! is dedicated to the members of the Junior League of Long Island, their families and their friends for their faithful contribution of recipes, their hours of cooking, their boundless enthusiasm and their cheerful cooperation . . . and

To Long Islanders here and elsewhere, who share this Island's fragile beauty and frantic pace and who join with us to create a community that sustains and nurtures all its members.

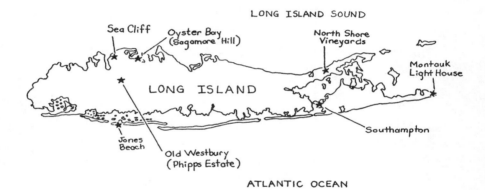

LONG ISLAND SOUND

Sea Cliff   Oyster Bay
(Sagamore Hill)

North Shore
Vineyards

Montauk
Light House

LONG ISLAND

Southampton

Jones
Beach

Old Westbury
(Phipps Estate)

ATLANTIC OCEAN

Acknowledgements

Special thanks to

Our professionals:

Polly Keener — artist and friend extraordinaire,
Chris Fox — for clever and pithy copy,
Cathy Hytner — for endless inputting,
Melanie May — for skilled editing,
Diane Weeks — for creative contribution,
Judith Carlson — for photographic resources

The Steering Committee, past and present, for counsel, commitment and stamina:

Ginny Martinez	Catherine Cooke
Kathy Nelson	Barbara Gopen
Crickett Byler-Martyn	Barbara Gifford
Suzanne Hess	Sabina McCarthy
Patricia Moore	Marie Munroe
Linda Langer	Celia Fraser
Becky Miller	Patricia Peters

The Presidents of the Junior League of Long Island:

Kathi Morse, Kathy Jeffers and Jody Masciandaro, under whose leadership this project was born, flourished and saw the light of day;

And to **Chery Manniello,** who chaired this project from beginning to end with vision, enthusiasm and dedication.

Foreword

The Junior League of Long Island celebrates thirty-nine years of community service with the publication of our cookbook, IT'S OUR SERVE!

Many people know **where** Long Island is; few who have not been here know **what** it is. Long a victim of stereotyping, the area is often symbolized by rows of tract houses and a traffic-snarled Long Island Expressway. But Long Island is so much more. Miles of world-famous beaches, distinguished vineyards, scenic roads and historic hamlets co-exist with heavily populated communities that offer an almost urban way of life. A network of golf courses, tennis courts, riding trails and playing fields dot nearly every village, leaving many visitors happily surprised. It is a region so diverse that it comfortably accommodates a population mix more common to city than country.

All of these elements have an impact on the way we live . . . and the way we cook! We are blessed by an abundance of fresh fish and local produce, have easy access to a wide range of interesting ingredients and point with pride to local wines of national distinction. We maintain an energetic lifestyle that precludes lengthy preparation, but makes creative use of the best of our local harvest.

Most of the recipes we are sharing here demand no complicated cooking skills — they require only your interest, enthusiasm and love of good food. They have been tested, re-tested, selected and edited in order to bring the best of Long Island to your table. We are proud to share them with you and happily announce, IT'S OUR SERVE!

The Junior League of Long Island

The Junior League of Long Island was founded in 1951 as the North Shore Junior Service League. In 1963, the name was changed to the Junior League of the North Shore, and in 1982, in a move designed to express a commitment to the entire community, the name became its present one.

Maintaining a thirty-nine-year tradition of service to Long Island, today's League reaches out to meet the needs of all Long Islanders through projects which address critical issues. **Lifeline**, a Junior League of Long Island publication, is a resource guide for Long Islanders who need assistance dealing with life-threatening illness; more than 15,000 copies have been distributed throughout the community. **Involvement Theater**, a League project for thirty years, annually brings live performances to between 3,000 and 5,000 emotionally and physically handicapped children who are in special schools all over Long Island. The **Hempstead Nursery Co-Op** is a respite care facility for parents who are at risk of abusing or neglecting their children. Offering assistance with vocational training, housing and parenting skills, the Co-op has helped change the future for the families enrolled.

These current projects reflect a strong tradition. The Junior League of Long Island points with pride to many social service agencies which began under Junior League of Long Island auspices and continue to flourish as independent organizations today: Family Service Association of Nassau County, Family Service League of Suffolk County, Child Abuse Prevention Services (CAPS) and the Center for Parents and Children at Glen Cove Hospital to name a few. The Junior League of Long Island was also instrumental in opening Long Island's first shelter for battered women and was one of the first organizations on Long Island to address the region's water crisis through a program of education and advocacy.

The Junior League of Long Island is supported by individual contributions, corporate and government funds. Recognizing that quality projects can succeed only if they have been adequately funded, the Junior League of Long Island has spent four years researching and developing this cookbook as an ongoing funding source. Revenues from IT'S OUR SERVE! will be used to maintain our League's high standards of community service.

Table of Contents

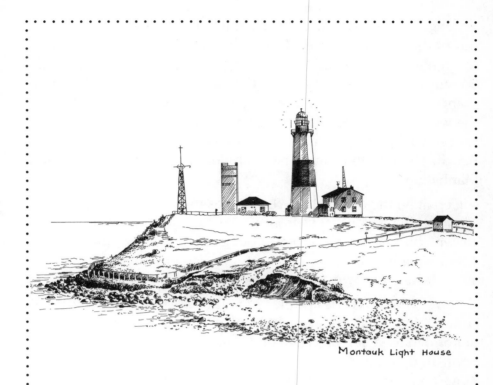

Montauk Light House

Appetizers

"Warming Up"

Long Island's shape has been likened to a whale swimming west out of the Atlantic Ocean. The bluffs and hills of the North Shore resemble the backbone, stretching the length of Long Island Sound; while the split tailfin is the North Fork, ending at Orient Point, and the South Fork, ending at Montauk Point. The belly of the whale is comprised of the sandy barrier islands — Fire Island, Jones Beach, Coney Island, Oak Island, Far Rockaway, and Long Beach. The mouth of the whale nibbles at our neighboring island, Manhattan.

Certainly, the appellation "Long" has never been disputed. Our Island stretches 120 miles from its west end near Manhattan to its eastern tip at Montauk Point. Four counties with a total area of 1,396 square miles make it the fourth-largest island in the U.S., after Hawaii and two Alaskan islands.

Long Island is definitely not the stereotypical "island" community, which one might expect to be cozy, compact and uniform in its style. Brooklyn and Queens, two of the five densely populated boroughs of New York City, appear on the map as Kings and Queens Counties. Our other two counties, Nassau and Suffolk, are commonly described as the "real" Long Island, where farmers produce the substantial bounty for Manhattan's and New York State's tables, and where the wealthy and not-so-wealthy escape the rigors of city life to enjoy the pleasures of country living.

Caviar Spread

6 hard-cooked eggs
3 tablespoons mayonnaise
1½ cups onion, minced
8 ounces cream cheese

⅔ cup sour cream
4 ounces well-drained caviar:
    ½ red, ½ black

Chop eggs and mix with mayonnaise. Spread mixture in a well greased 8-inch springform pan. Sprinkle onions over egg mixture.

Soften cream cheese and blend with sour cream until smooth. Spread this mixture over onions with wet spatula.

Chill 3 hours or overnight. Top creatively with well drained caviar. Serve with crackers or toast points.

Serves: 20
Special Equipment: 8-inch Springform Pan

For Christmas, use all red caviar and garnish with fresh holly leaves.

Caviar Eclairs

Pâté a choux:

1 cup water
4 tablespoons butter
¼ teaspoon salt
1 cup flour

4 eggs
1 egg yolk
2 tablespoons water

Filling:

6 ounces sliced, smoked salmon, pre-packaged
8 ounces whipped cream cheese
½ cup dairy sour cream

2 to 3 ounces black caviar
Fresh dill, finely chopped
Freshly ground pepper to taste

Preheat oven to 350 degrees. To make Pâté a choux, combine water, butter, and salt in a medium saucepan (not non-stick), bring to a boil. Remove from heat. Add flour all at once and stir until combined.

Return to medium/low heat and "dry" for 5 to 6 minutes until a layer of dough sticks to the bottom of the pan and the pastry does not stick to your fingers when pinched. Cool for 10 minutes.

Beat in eggs one at a time. Beat well after each addition until pastry is yellow and glossy. Butter and flour a large baking sheet.

Spoon pastry into a piping bag fitted with a large tip. Pipe onto baking sheet in 2-inch long strips, two layers deep. Brush eclairs with milk or an egg wash made from 1 egg yolk and 2 tablespoons of water. Reshape as necessary. Let sit for another 20 minutes.

Continued on next page

Bake at 350 degrees for 20 minutes until brown. (Do not open the oven too often). Turn off oven, open door a crack, and let eclairs sit for an hour or so. At this point they are ready to fill.

Filling: Cut salmon into 1½-inch lengths and as wide as eclairs. Split open eclairs, spread with a thin layer of cream cheese on the bottom of eclair and lay a piece of salmon on the cheese.

Spread a thin layer of sour cream on the salmon and top with a dab of caviar.

Sprinkle with dill and freshly ground black pepper.

Return the tops to the eclairs and serve immediately.

Yield: 20 Pieces

Crab Mold

2 envelopes unflavored gelatin
¼ cup cold water
8 ounces cream cheese
1 can cream of mushroom soup
1 cup mayonnaise
1 teaspoon Worcestershire sauce
1 small onion, chopped

1 cup celery, chopped
8 ounces crabmeat, fresh or
   canned, drained and shredded
Juice of 1 lemon
Dash fresh pepper
1 teaspoon fresh parsley,
   chopped

Dissolve gelatin in water. Set aside.

In top of double boiler put cream cheese, soup, mayonnaise, and Worcestershire sauce.

Stir over moderate heat until all is mixed. Cool slightly.

Add onion, celery, crabmeat, lemon juice, pepper, parsley, and gelatin. Stir well.

Spoon into 3-cup mold and refrigerate for 2 to 3 hours.

Unmold and serve with crackers.

Serves: 10 to 12
Special Equipment: Double boiler / 3-cup mold

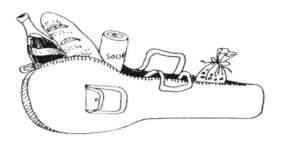

Gravlax

2 pounds salmon, in 2 pieces with skin on

1 bunch fresh dill, or a jar of dried

2 tablespoons sugar

3 tablespoons salt

1 teaspoon white pepper

Small slices of black bread, if desired

Sauce:

3 tablespoons Swedish mustard

2 tablespoons French mustard

2 tablespoons sugar

4 tablespoons vinegar

½ cup oil

Dill, minced

Wash and dry salmon; be certain all small bones are removed. Mix all the spices together. Put ¼ of the spice mixture in the bottom of a baking dish large enough to hold the salmon.

Place first piece of salmon into dish, skin side down. Sprinkle ⅓ of the remaining spices on the fleshy side of fish; then ⅓ on fleshy side of second piece of fish. Place 2 pieces of fish, fleshy sides together, in pan and top with last ⅓ of spice mixture.

Rest a cutting board and something heavy (such as canned vegetables) on top of fish and let marinate in refrigerator for 48 hours, turning fish over every 12 hours.

To serve, scrape off spices and cut salmon into thin slices. Can be served on sliced black bread with the following sauce.

Sauce: In a food processor, combine mustards, sugar, and vinegar. Slowly pour in oil until it is thoroughly incorporated. Add more sugar to taste. Stir in 2 tablespoons minced dill.

Serves: 6

Smoked Salmon Rollups

2 pounds smoked salmon, thinly
    sliced
1 teaspoon lemon juice per slice
1 tablespoon olive oil per slice

Freshly ground black pepper, to
    taste
Small capers

Spread each slice of smoked salmon with olive oil. Sprinkle with lemon juice, black pepper, and a few capers. Roll up and chill.

Cut into bite-sized pieces and serve. Garnish with lemon wedges.

Serves: 10

Salmon Mousse

1 envelope unflavored gelatin
Juice of whole lemon
1 small onion
½ cup boiling water
½ cup mayonnaise
1 teaspoon paprika

1 teaspoon white pepper
1 teaspoon salt
1 teaspoon red vinegar
1 pound salmon (1 large can)
1 cup heavy cream

Empty gelatin into blender. Add lemon juice, onion, and boiling water. Blend at high speed for 40 seconds. Add mayonnaise, paprika, salt, pepper, vinegar, and salmon. Blend.

In a separate bowl, whip cream to form a peak. Fold blender mixture into whipped cream. Pour into an oiled mold and chill.

Serves: 10
Special Equipment: Blender

Pickled Marinated Scallops

¾ pound scallops

4 small white onions, sliced

Small bunch fresh dill, finely chopped

1 tablespoon pickling spice

1 tablespoon dill seed

½ tablespoon sugar

½ tablespoon salt

2 tablespoons oil

¾ cup white vinegar

2¼ cups water

Two or 3 days before serving, place scallops and onions in a glass bowl. Mix remaining ingredients (three pinches of dill bunch only) in a saucepan and simmer 15 minutes. Remove from heat and allow to cool 5 minutes.

Pour saucepan ingredients through a sieve over scallops and onions. Allow to cool to room temperature. Stir and refrigerate.

When ready to serve, drain scallops, and sprinkle remaining chopped fresh dill over them.

Serves: 8

Try serving this with a variety of mustards.

Crab Spread

8 ounces frozen crabmeat, thawed

8 ounces cream cheese, softened

4 tablespoons heavy cream

2 tablespoons onion, chopped

½ teaspoon horseradish

Salt and pepper

½ cup sliced almonds

Mix all ingredients together, except almonds. Put in greased casserole dish. Cover with sliced almonds. Bake at 350 degrees for 30 minutes. Serve with crackers, bread sticks, or melba toast.

Artichoke and Shrimp Boat

1 egg yolk

¾ cup olive oil

¼ cup wine vinegar

2 tablespoons Dijon mustard

1 shallot, finely chopped

2 tablespoons parsley

2 tablespoons chives

2 8½-ounce cans artichoke hearts, drained

1 pound medium shrimp, cooked and cleaned

1 loaf French bread, center scooped out and discarded

Mix egg yolk, olive oil, wine vinegar, mustard, shallot, parsley, and chives together. Pour over shrimp and artichoke hearts.

Make a day ahead and keep in refrigerator covered, stirring occasionally. Spoon mixture into prepared bread. Serve with raw vegetables or crackers.

Grilled Spicy Shrimp

2 pounds large shrimp, deveined,
   split in half lengthwise

4 juniper berries, crushed
   (optional)

¼ cup gin

Juice of 1 lemon

Juice of 1 lime

⅛ teaspoon crushed red pepper

Sauce:

1 tablespoon fresh ginger (or to
   taste), grated

½ cup apricot jam

¼ cup orange marmalade

1 tablespoon fresh dill, chopped

Pinch crushed red pepper

Combine shrimp, juniper berries, gin, lemon juice, lime juice, and crushed red pepper. Stir and marinate shrimp for at least 4 hours or overnight.

Split shrimp in half and skewer each piece. Grill or cook at 425 degrees for about 5 minutes. Mix all ingredients for sauce.

Serve shrimp with sauce on the side.

Serves: 10

Special Equipment: Wooden skewers

Chinese Chicken Wings

. . . .

1½ cups soy sauce
¾ cup sherry
1 cup Hoisin sauce*
¾ cup plum sauce*
18 green onions, chopped

¾ cup cider vinegar
½ cup honey
6 to 7 pounds chicken wings,
  split at joint

Mix first seven ingredients in saucepan. Bring to a boil and boil hard for 5 minutes.

Cool. Pour over chicken wings and marinate in refrigerator for 24 hours.

Drain chicken wings and bake at 325 degrees for 1½ hours. Baste with marinade every 20 minutes.

Garnish with thinly sliced scallions and serve at room temperature.

Serves: 20

This is a terrific buffet dish.

* available in gourmet or Oriental section of supermarket

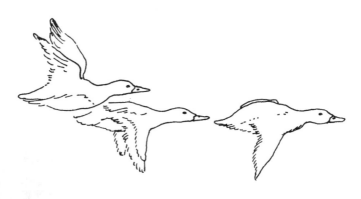

. . . .

Turkey Pâté Endive

1 cup walnuts, toasted

2 cups fresh smoked turkey, cut in chunks

¼ cup unsalted butter, softened

½ cup mayonnaise

½ cup sour cream

1 tablespoon scallions, minced

6 heads Belgian endive

Grapes for garnish

Chop walnuts in food processor for 3 or 4 minutes. Add remaining ingredients (except endive and grapes) and continue processing until finely ground. Cover and chill up to 24 hours.

To serve, separate endive leaves. Spoon pâté at leaf bottom and arrange leaves on round tray.

Garnish with grapes and serve.

Serves: 4 to 5
Special Equipment: Food Processor

Chicken Liver Pâté

½ pound butter
1 pound chicken livers
½ clove garlic
¼ small onion

⅛ teaspoon basil
2 tablespoons cognac
Salt and pepper to taste

Melt ¼ pound of butter in a skillet. Sauté liver quickly, until brown on the outside, but still pink in the middle (about 5 minutes). Partly cover pan. Allow livers to cool, until butter just starts to set, turning livers several times to prevent darkening.

Place livers in blender. Add remaining butter (softened to room temperature) and remaining ingredients. Blend until smooth, pushing down with a spatula.

Adjust seasonings and put in a well buttered 1 quart mold. Cover and refrigerate. Unmold and serve with crackers.

Serves: 12
Special Equipment: 1 quart mold/Blender

Curry Mayonnaise Dip

1 cup mayonnaise
¼ teaspoon ginger
1 teaspoon curry powder

¼ teaspoon garlic powder
1 teaspoon honey
1 tablespoon lemon juice

Blend all ingredients together.

Serve as a dip for raw vegtables or shrimp, or with kiwi and pineapple for a light dessert.

Serves: 8 to 10

Crudité Dip

1 cup mayonnaise
2 teaspoons tarragon vinegar
Dash white pepper
½ teaspoon salt
2 tablespoons onion, grated
⅛ teaspoon thyme

1 teaspoon curry powder
2 teaspoons chives, chopped
1 teaspoon chili sauce
1 teaspoon ketchup
Pinch horseradish

Put ingredients in bowl and mix well with whisk.

Garnish with paprika and/or parsley.

Serves: 6

Hot Artichoke Dip

1 14-ounce can artichoke hearts, finely chopped

1 cup mayonnaise

1 cup Parmesan cheese

1 cup mozzarella cheese, shredded

1 teaspoon Tabasco sauce

½ teaspoon salt

Combine all ingredients and mix thoroughly. Put into 1½-quart ovenproof dish and bake at 350 degrees for 30 minutes. Serve warm with crackers.

Serves: 12

Mock Boursin

12 ounces cream cheese at room temperature

8 ounces butter at room temperature

¼ teaspoon salt

¼ teaspoon pepper

¼ teaspoon garlic powder

¼ teaspoon dill

¼ teaspoon marjoram

¼ teaspoon thyme

¼ teaspoon basil

¼ teaspoon oregano

Cream together cream cheese and butter in food processor. Add seasonings and mix well. Serve with crackers and/or vegetables.

Yield: 2 cups
Special Equipment: Food Processor

Make a double batch and freeze.

Spinach Cheese Balls

2 10-ounce packages frozen
  chopped spinach
1 tablespoon minced dried onion
2 cups herb-seasoned stuffing
  mix

1 cup grated Parmesan cheese
2 eggs, beaten
3 tablespoons butter, melted

In a saucepan, cook spinach according to package directions. Drain and add dried onion.

In a mixing bowl, combine spinach mixture, stuffing, and cheese. Stir in eggs and melted butter. Let stand for 15 minutes.

Shape into 1-inch balls. Place in a shallow ovenproof pan. Bake at 375 degrees for 10 to 15 minutes or until heated through.

Yield: 48

This can also be made in a 9-inch pie pan and cut into wedges as a luncheon dish.

Red Peppers and Mozzarella with Basil

8 tablespoons olive oil

4 tablespoons red wine vinegar

2 cloves garlic, crushed

3 tablespoons basil paste (pesto)

Salt and freshly ground pepper to taste

6 red peppers, roasted, peeled, halved lengthwise; or 3 jars roasted peppers

1 package (16 ounces) mozzarella

1 small red onion, thinly sliced

Anchovy filets (optional)

1 loaf Italian bread, sliced

Prepare vinaigrette: Combine oil, vinegar, garlic, basil paste, salt, and pepper in jar. Cover and shake until well blended. Set aside.

On a rectangular serving platter make an overlapping pattern of red peppers, slices of mozzarella, and sliced onions. Pour vinaigrette over this. Marinate 3 to 6 hours.

Just before serving, garnish with anchovy filets and serve slightly chilled or at room temperature with Italian bread.

Serves: 6 to 8

Hot Brie

. . . .

8-inch round of Brie　　　　　　　　　**1 cup pecans, chopped or whole**
2 cups brown sugar

Preheat broiler.

Cut crust from side and top of cheese and place Brie in a 10-inch quiche or pie plate. Cover top and sides with sugar, patting gently. Sprinkle pecans on top. Broil on lowest rack until sugar bubbles and melts, about 3 minutes.

Garnish with fresh apple wedges.

Serves: 10
Special Equipment: 10-inch pie plate

. . . .

Pepperoni Stuffed Mushrooms

12 large mushrooms

2 tablespoons butter or margarine

1 medium onion, finely chopped

½ cup pepperoni, diced

¼ cup green pepper, finely chopped

1 small clove garlic, minced

½ cup snack crackers, finely crushed

3 tablespoons Parmesan cheese, grated

1 tablespoon fresh parsley, finely chopped

½ teaspoon salt

¼ teaspoon dried oregano

Dash pepper

⅓ cup chicken broth

Set aside mushroom caps. Chop stems.

Sauté onion, pepperoni, green pepper, garlic, and mushroom stems in butter.

Combine crackers, Parmesan cheese, parsley, salt, oregano, and pepper and add to sautéed vegetables and pepperoni.

Spoon mixture into caps and place in baking dish. Add broth to baking dish and bake uncovered at 325 degrees for 25 minutes.

Serves: 6

Mushrooms Croustadier

Sliced white bread
4 tablespoons butter, unsalted
3 tablespoons shallots, chopped
¾ pound mushrooms, sliced
2 teaspoons flour
1 cup heavy cream

½ teaspoon salt
Dash cayenne
1½ tablespoons chives
½ teaspoon lemon juice
1 tablespoon parsley, chopped
½ cup Parmesan cheese

Cut 3-inch rounds from white bread and press into buttered mini muffin tin and bake for 10 minutes at 400 degrees.

Melt butter and sauté shallots and mushrooms. Drain, remove from heat, sprinkle with flour and stir. Return to heat and add ¾ cup of cream, stirring constantly. Bring to a boil and then simmer for 1 to 2 minutes. Remove from heat and stir in ¼ cup of cream, salt, cayenne, chives, lemon juice, and parsley. Cool.

Fill croustade (bread) shells with mushroom mixture, mounding slightly. Sprinkle with grated Parmesan cheese and bake at 350 degrees for 10 minutes. Broil for 5 seconds if desired.

Serves: 10
Special Equipment: Mini muffin tins

Pickled Mushrooms

⅓ cup dry white wine

⅓ cup white wine vinegar

⅓ cup salad oil

¼ cup onion or shallots, finely chopped

2 tablespoons fresh parsley, snipped

1 small clove garlic, peeled

1 bay leaf

1 teaspoon salt

¼ teaspoon thyme

Dash ground pepper

12 ounces canned whole mushrooms, drained

In saucepan, combine all ingredients except mushrooms. Bring to a boil. Add mushrooms and return to a boil.

Lower heat and simmer, uncovered, 8 to 10 minutes. Cool and store in covered container in refrigerator until ready to serve.

Yield: 1 pint

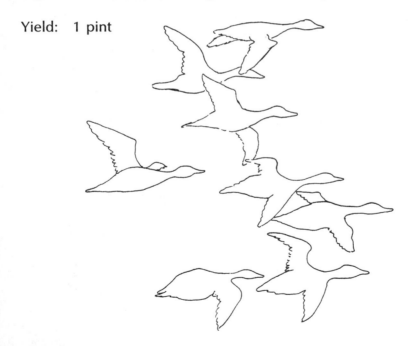

Marinated Italian Dried Tomatoes

½ pound Italian dried tomatoes
½ cup extra virgin olive oil
4 large cloves garlic, crushed in
   press

5 tablespoons balsamic vinegar
Freshly ground pepper

Put dried tomatoes in glass jar.

Combine all remaining ingredients in small bowl and whisk. Pour marinade over tomatoes. Shake jar until all tomatoes are coated. Store for 3 months. Invert jar or give it a shake whenever you notice it.

Yield: 1 quart
Special Equipment: Quart glass jar with tight lid

While it seems an incredibly long time to wait for the first jar, you may never have to wait again. Start a new jar each time the "useful" jar is ⅔ empty.

Eggplant Caviar

. . . .

2 large eggplants
2 tablespoons oil
2 large onions, finely chopped
2 cloves garlic, finely chopped
2 medium green peppers, finely chopped

2 cans (6 ounces each) tomato paste
2 teaspoons white vinegar
Salt and pepper to taste
Thin slices pumpernickel bread

Preheat oven to 425 degrees.

Place eggplants on rack in center of oven. Cook for an hour, turning a few times. Eggplants should be soft and skin should be blistered. Remove skin from eggplants and chop meat fine.

Heat oil and cook onions, garlic, and green peppers until soft, not brown. Add tomato paste and simmer 3 to 5 minutes. Stir in vinegar, salt, pepper and chopped eggplant. Cook for 30 minutes in skillet at low heat.

Cool thoroughly, then chill. Serve on pumpernickel slices.

Serves: 8 to 10

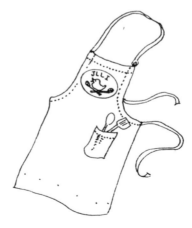

. . . .

Spinach Bread Canapés

1 package (1 pound) frozen
    bread dough

1 pound sweet sausage (4 to 5
    links)

1 medium onion, chopped

12 ounces fresh mushrooms,
    sliced

10-ounce package frozen
    chopped spinach, thawed

1 cup cheddar cheese, grated

Thaw dough. Let rise and punch down once. Divide in half and roll out to about ½-inch thickness.

Remove casings from sausage and brown with onion and mushrooms.

Drain spinach well and add to sausage and onion. Simmer until most of moisture is gone. Remove from heat and stir in cheese.

Grease small cookie sheet and spread out half of dough on sheet.

Spoon spinach mixture on top of dough and pat down with a fork. Cover with remaining dough, crimping edges and making a few fork marks on top of the dough for decoration.

Bake at 350 degrees until dough is golden brown. Cut into serving sized pieces and serve warm.

Serves: 20

Hummus

. . . .

2 cups chick peas (garbanzo
  beans), rinsed and drained

1 teaspoon salt

½ cup cold water

3 medium cloves garlic, peeled
  and pressed

¼ cup fresh lemon juice

⅔ cup tahini (sesame paste)

Pita bread

Place first six ingredients in a blender. Blend until smooth. Use as a
dip with toasted pita bread cut into triangles or with fresh vegetables.

Serves: 12
Special Equipment: Blender/Food Processor

Layered Mexican Dip

. . . .

2 ripe avocados, mashed

1 cup sour cream

¾ package taco seasoning mix

6 ounces sharp cheddar cheese,
  grated

6 ounces jalapeño jack cheese,
  grated

1 bunch scallions, minced

1 10-ounce can pitted black
  olives, sliced

3 medium tomatoes, diced

Mix sour cream and taco seasoning mix until well blended.

In large glass bowl with flat bottom, layer ingredients in the order
listed. Serve with tortilla chips.

Serves: 10

. . . .

Chile Con Queso

1 cup American cheese, cubed
½ cup cheddar cheese, grated
¼ cup light cream or evaporated milk

1 medium tomato, chopped
1 frozen or canned green chile, chopped (optional)
⅛ teaspoon garlic powder

To Double:

1 pound American cheese, cubed
10 ounces cheddar cheese, grated
½ cup light cream or evaporated milk

2 to 3 tomatoes, chopped
Small can chile peppers, chopped
¼ teaspoon garlic powder

Melt cheeses together being careful not to burn. Add cream or evaporated milk, stirring constantly. Add rest of ingredients and more cream as desired.

Serve hot (use chafing dish or fondue pot) with tortilla chips. Garnish with the bottom section of a bright red bell pepper placed in the center of the dip.

Serves: 8 to 10
Special Equipment: Fondue pot / Chafing dish

This freezes very well.

Honey Mustard Palmiers

1 sheet frozen puff pastry
3 tablespoons honey mustard
4 ounces prosciutto
1 cup grated Parmesan cheese

1 egg
2 teaspoons water
Parchment sheets

Preheat oven to 400 degrees.

Place puff pastry on work surface and roll to 18×11 inches. Spread honey mustard over top. Arrange prosciutto over mustard to cover pastry. Sprinkle with cheese.

Starting at one long edge, roll pastry jelly-roll style to middle. Repeat with other side.

Using a serrated knife, cut crosswise into ½-inch slices. Place on parchment-lined cookie sheets and press lightly to flatten.

Refrigerate 15 minutes. Beat egg with water, brush tops of palmiers with egg wash.

Bake for 10 minutes. Serve warm or at room temperature.

Serves: 8

Crispy Potato Skins

6 medium potatoes, baked
Melted butter
Salt
Pepper

¼ cup Parmesan cheese, grated
¼ cup mozzarella cheese, grated
1 teaspoon oregano
⅛ teaspoon garlic powder

Preheat oven to 400 degrees.

Cut each potato lengthwise into 4 quarters. Scoop out pulp from shells leaving ⅛-inch shell.

Brush inside and out with melted butter and sprinkle with salt and pepper. Place skin side down on baking sheet.

Mix remaining ingredients and sprinkle over potatoes.

Bake in preheated oven for 20 to 25 minutes or until crisp.

Serves: 4 to 6

Serve with sour cream for dipping.

Basil Bread Canapés

1 package frozen pizza dough

2 cups fresh basil leaves

⅓ cup olive oil

⅓ cup pine nuts or walnuts, toasted lightly under broiler

2 cloves garlic

1 teaspoon salt

½ teaspoon freshly ground pepper

2 ounces Parmesan cheese, grated

1 ounce Romano cheese, grated

½ cup mozzarella cheese, shredded

The night before or early in the morning, oil a large bowl and place frozen pizza dough in it. Cover with oiled plastic wrap. Set in a draft-free place for several hours to rise.

Combine basil, oil, nuts, garlic, salt, and pepper in food processor until well mixed.

Punch down dough and spread on oiled pizza pan or cookie sheet.

Stir Parmesan and Romano cheese into basil sauce and spoon sauce evenly over dough. Top with mozzarella.

Bake in preheated 400 degree oven for 20 to 25 minutes.

Cut into 2-inch squares and serve.

Serves: 8 to 10
Special Equipment: Food Processor

Mary's Pesto Pâté

2 8-ounce packages cream
  cheese

2½ cups sweet butter

1 cup sun dried tomatoes,
  chopped

1 cup pesto sauce (see Pesto
  Pizza recipe on page 40, or
  purchase ready-made)

Allow butter and cream cheese to soften, then mix well in food processor.

Oil 4 cup mold and spread one third of cream cheese and butter mixture on bottom of mold. Spread sun dried tomatoes over cheese.

Top with second third of cream cheese mixture, then cover this with pesto sauce, taking care not to place pesto too near the sides.

Top with final third of cream cheese mixture, cover and refrigerate.

Unmold and serve with bagel strips or crackers.

Serves: 8 to 12
Special Equipment: Food Processor / 4 cup mold

Pesto Pizza

2 cups fresh basil leaves

½ teaspoon salt

½ teaspoon pepper

1 tablespoon garlic, chopped

2 tablespoons pignoli nuts, chopped

½ cup (or more) olive oil

½ cup Parmesan cheese, freshly grated

Pizza dough, approximately 1 pound to make 2 pies

1 pound mozzarella cheese, grated

Egg beaten with 1 tablespoon water

To make pesto sauce, combine first 5 ingredients in food processor. Slowly blend in oil, adding more if paste seems too thick. Put into bowl and stir in Parmesan cheese. (Any leftover sauce keeps well either refrigerated or frozen.)

To make pizza dough, roll out pizza dough into 2, 15-inch rounds and brush with egg mixture almost to edge. Pinch up sides to form a rim. Spread each with one half of the pesto sauce and sprinkle with mozzarella cheese. Let stand for about 30 minutes before cooking.

Preheat pizza stone for 20 minutes in a 425 degree oven or bake on a cookie sheet. Lower temperature to 400 degrees and bake pizza until dough is golden and cheese has melted.

Serves: 16 or More

Special Equipment: Food Processor / Pizza stone

East End Windmill

Soups & Chowders

"The First Serve"

The recorded history of Long Island began in the early 1600s with Henry Hudson's brief landing. The English first settled at the eastern end of Long Island in 1639 on Gardiner's Island, and western Long Island greeted European colonists in Hempstead in 1643. Long before these colonial visitors arrived, however, this beautiful and bountiful Island had been home to Indians related to the Algonquins of the eastern seaboard.

The first settlers encountered the loosely connected thirteen tribes of Paumanok, meaning "land of tribute," and referring to the payments these peaceful Indians made annually to prevent invasion by their more warlike relatives on the mainland. Many of the names of these thirteen tribes appear as town names on the map of Long Island: Rockaway, Manhasset, Massapequa, Shinnecock, and Montauk are a few examples.

By 1776, the American spirit of the thirteen original colonies was strong on the Island. Three Long Islanders were signers of the Declaration of Independence. The Battle of Long Island was the first major confrontation of the Revolutionary War and resulted in British occupation of Long Island until the Treaty of Paris in 1783.

Cries of "Liberty!" changed to "Whale Ho!" on Long Island in the first half of the 1800s. Sag Harbor and Cold Spring Harbor became thriving centers of the whaling industry, which did not decline until petroleum began to replace whale oil for lighting in the 1860s. Today, Long Island has two fine whaling museums that recall this era.

Apple Curry Soup

. . . .

2 large apples, cored, peeled,
   and sliced

2 teaspoons curry powder

2 medium onions, peeled and
   diced

2 10½ ounce cans beef
   consommé

1 pint heavy cream

Salt and pepper to taste

Combine apples, onions, and consommé in saucepan. Simmer 30 minutes, cool, and strain. Reserve a few apple slices for garnish.

Heat cream slowly in double boiler. Add strained soup, curry powder, salt, and pepper. Chill several hours before serving. Garnish with apple slices.

Serves: 4
Special Equipment: Double boiler

Cold Peach Soup

. . . .

2 pounds peaches, peeled, pitted,
   and sliced

2½ cups sour cream

1 cup fresh orange juice

1 cup pineapple juice

½ cup dry sherry

1 tablespoon fresh lime juice

Purée peaches in food processor until smooth. Add remaining ingredients gradually and blend well. Serve chilled. Garnish with mint sprig, unpeeled peach slice or lime slice.

Serves: 8
Special Equipment: Food Processor

. . . .

Carrot Soup

15 carrots
4 potatoes
3 tablespoons butter
¾ cup onion, chopped
6 cups chicken broth
1 teaspoon dried thyme
1 bay leaf

1½ cups heavy cream
⅛ teaspoon Tabasco sauce
½ teaspoon Worcestershire sauce
½ teaspoon sugar
Salt and pepper to taste
1 cup whole milk

Peel carrots and potatoes. Cut into small pieces. Set aside.

Heat butter in soup kettle. Add onion and stir. Cook briefly. Add vegetables, bay leaf, thyme, and broth. Bring to boil, reduce heat to simmer and cook 35 minutes or until vegetables are tender. Cool. Remove bay leaf.

Blend in food processor or electric blender in three batches. Return to kettle. Bring to boil and add remaining ingredients.

Serve piping hot or chilled. Garnish with fresh parsley or chives.

Serves: 8
Special Equipment: Food Processor/Blender

Tamah's Cheese Soup

1 chicken bouillon cube
1 beef bouillon cube
1½ cups water
1 clove garlic
3 carrots
¾ cup onions, chopped
15 green beans, frozen or fresh

1 zucchini, sliced into ¼-inch slices
10-ounce can cream of mushroom soup
10-ounce can cream of chicken soup
1 to 1½ cups milk
¾ pound grated cheddar cheese

Heat water and dissolve bouillon cubes.

In blender or food processor, finely chop garlic, carrots, onions, green beans, and zucchini.

Add chopped vegetables to dissolved bouillon and cook until done, about 10 minutes.

Add cream soups and stir in 1 cup milk; add balance of milk after soups are thoroughly blended.

Add grated cheese and cook over low heat until cheese melts.

Serve with French bread croutons.

Serves: 6 to 8
Special Equipment: Blender/Food Processor

Cream of Chicken Soup

3 tablespoons butter or
margarine
2 tablespoons flour
7 cups chicken broth
Chicken carcass

1 onion, finely chopped
1 carrot, finely chopped
1 celery stalk, finely chopped
2 egg yolks
½ cup light cream

Melt butter in large saucepan. Add flour and stir. Remove from heat.

Heat 1 cup of broth and add at once to flour/butter mixture. Stir with wire whisk until thick. Add rest of broth, carcass, and vegetables. Simmer uncovered for 1 hour.

Remove carcass, strain soup, and return to clean saucepan. Combine yolks and cream and add to soup.

Do not boil! Serve immediately.

Serves: 6

Long Island Clam Chowder

1 peck (8 quarts) chowder clams

4 ribs celery, trimmed and cut into 2-inch lengths

½ pound small onions, quartered

1 pound peeled potatoes, quartered

2 large carrots, peeled, trimmed, and cut into 1-inch lengths

1 pound peeled tomatoes (canned or fresh), chopped

6 tablespoons butter

½ cup parsley, chopped

4 cups heavy cream

Salt and freshly ground pepper

Open raw clams. Retain all clam meat and juices. This should result in 1 quart of clams and 6 to 8 cups of clam juice. Set juice aside.

Rinse each clam under cold running water. Trim away black part of clam and discard. Put celery, onions, potatoes and carrots in food processor and process to a medium chop. Place mixture in heavy pot and add tomatoes.

Process clams briefly in processor. Add clams to vegetables. Add clam juice and bring to boil. Cook uncovered about 2 hours, skimming off surface if necessary. Stir in butter and parsley.

When chowder is ready to serve, remove from heat and add heavy cream with salt and pepper to taste. Bring just to a boil. Do not boil chowder or it will curdle. Serve hot.

Serves: 10 to 12
Special Equipment: Food Processor

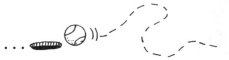

New England Clam Chowder

3 10-ounce cans minced clams
Water
½ pound lean salt pork, diced
1 cup onion, chopped
3 cups potatoes, peeled and
    diced

1 teaspoon salt
¼ teaspoon white pepper
2 cups light cream
2 cups milk
2 tablespoons butter
Paprika

Strain and reserve liquid from clams. Measure liquid and add enough water to make 4 cups.

Fry pork in large kettle until golden. Remove pork and reserve. Drain off all but ¼ cup fat. Add onions to fat and sauté for 5 minutes. Add potatoes, salt, pepper, and clam liquid. Simmer until potatoes are tender. Add clams, cream, milk, and butter. Reheat, but do not boil.

Top with crisp pork and sprinkle with paprika.

Yield: 3 quarts

Crab and Asparagus Soup

½ cup butter
¼ cup all purpose flour
4 cups milk
2 tablespoons onion, chopped
3 teaspoons chicken bouillon
  powder
2 teaspoons fresh parsley,
  chopped

½ teaspoon pepper
½ teaspoon grated nutmeg
½ pound fresh backfin crabmeat,
  or 2 6½-ounce cans backfin
  crab
1 pound fresh asparagus, peeled
  and cut into 1-inch pieces

In a saucepan, melt butter, whisk in flour, and cook 3 minutes. Add milk, whisk until smooth.

Add onions, bouillon, parsley, pepper, and nutmeg.

Bring to boil, reduce heat and simmer until soup thickens, about 5 minutes stirring constantly.

Add crabmeat and cook until soup is creamy, about 10 minutes.

Add asparagus and cook until it is tender-crisp, about 2 or 3 minutes. Serve hot.

Serves: 6 to 8

Gazpacho

1 cup fresh tomatoes, chopped

½ cup green pepper, chopped

½ cup celery, chopped

½ cup cucumber, peeled and chopped

¼ cup onion, chopped

2 teaspoons parsley, chopped

1 teaspoon chives, chopped

1 small garlic clove, minced

2 to 3 tablespoons tarragon vinegar

2 tablespoons olive oil

1 teaspoon salt

¼ teaspoon pepper

½ teaspoon Worcestershire sauce

2 cups vegetable tomato juice

Combine all ingredients. Chill 4 hours. Serve cold. Garnish with a dollop of sour cream or sprig of parsley.

Serves: 6

Cold Cucumber Soup

4 or 5 scallions, finely chopped

1½ heaping tablespoons dried pea soup

1 pint half and half

Salt and pepper to taste

1 tablespoon Worcestershire sauce

Dash Tabasco

6 ounces chicken broth

2 large cucumbers, peeled

Put all ingredients except cucumber into blender and mix well.

Cut cucumbers into large chunks. Add to mixture in blender. Process only long enough to thoroughly mix cucumber into liquid ingredients. Cucumber should be crunchy, not finely diced. Adjust seasonings and chill. Garnish with slice of lemon, fresh parsley, or chives.

Serves: 4 to 6
Special Equipment: Blender

Lobster Bisque

2 1½-pound lobsters
6 tablespoons unsalted butter
⅓ cup cognac
¾ cup shallots, chopped
3 cloves garlic, minced
3 tablespoons tomato paste
2½ cups white wine
1 teaspoon dried tarragon

½ teaspoon thyme
Dash red pepper flakes
2 bay leaves
3 tablespoons flour
2 cups milk
1 cup heavy cream
Salt and pepper to taste

Boil lobster for 20 minutes. Remove meat from lobster and dice. Reserve 4 cups of cooking water.

Melt 3 tablespoons butter in large skillet. Pour in cognac and heat until cognac is warm.

Stir in shallots, garlic, tomato paste, wine, reserved lobster cooking water, tarragon, thyme, pepper flakes, and bay leaves. Simmer uncovered for 30 minutes. Strain into a bowl.

Melt 3 tablespoons butter in large pot. Add flour and cook, whisking constantly for 1 minute. Gradually whisk in strained vegetable and spice mixture. Stir until well blended.

Whisk in milk and cream. Heat thoroughly. Add salt and pepper to taste. Stir in reserved lobster meat and cook until heated through. Serve immediately.

Serves: 6

Minestrone Soup

3 tablespoons olive oil

4 to 5 cloves garlic, crushed

1 cup onion, chopped

1 teaspoon salt (optional)

1 cup carrots, chopped

1 cup celery, minced

1 cup eggplant or zucchini, peeled and cubed

1 teaspoon oregano

¼ teaspoon black pepper

1 teaspoon basil

1 cup green pepper, chopped

4 cups water or soup stock

2 cups tomato purée

1½ cups garbanzo beans (chick peas)

3 tablespoons dry red wine

1 cup tomatoes, chopped

½ cup uncooked pasta (tiny shells are best)

Parsley

6 tablespoons fresh Parmesan cheese, grated

In soup kettle, sauté garlic and onions in olive oil until they are soft and translucent. Add salt, carrots, celery, and eggplant. (If you use zucchini, add it with the green pepper.) Mix well. Add oregano, black pepper, and basil. Cover and cook over moderate heat for 5 to 8 minutes.

Add green pepper, stock, tomato purée, garbanzo beans, and wine. Cover and simmer for 15 minutes.

Add tomatoes. Keep at very low heat until 10 minutes before serving.

Just before serving, heat to boiling, add pasta, and boil gently until pasta is tender.

Top with parsley and Parmesan cheese and serve immediately.

Serves: 8 to 12

Mushroom Soup

½ pound fresh mushrooms, thinly
   sliced
3 tablespoons butter
1 teaspoon salt
Freshly ground pepper to taste

2 cups chicken broth
1½ cups heavy cream
2 egg yolks
Chopped parsley

Sauté sliced mushrooms in butter until golden brown. Add salt, pepper, and broth. Simmer for 15 minutes. Mix egg yolks with cream and add to soup. Stir constantly until slightly thickened. Garnish with parsley.

Serves: 4

Radish Soup

2 tablespoons safflower oil
¼ cup onion, chopped
5 bunches radishes
4 cups chicken broth

1 cup light cream or milk
Sour cream
1 scallion, chopped

In medium saucepan, sauté onion in oil until it is translucent. Clean radishes and add to onions. Cover with chicken broth. Bring to boil. Lower heat and simmer about 15 minutes until radishes are tender.

Purée in food processor. Return to pan. Add cream and reheat gently. Serve warm or chilled with dollop of sour cream and chopped scallions.

Serves: 4 to 6
Special Equipment: Food Processor

Country-Style Onion Soup

1 tablespoon bacon drippings
  (butter can be substituted)
4 large onions, finely chopped
2 teaspoons flour
½ teaspoon salt
⅛ teaspoon pepper
1 clove garlic, mashed
Pinch of parsley

Pinch of thyme
1 quart chicken stock
1 cup dry white wine
1 teaspoon cognac (optional)
French bread
Grated Parmesan cheese
½ cup butter, melted

In deep saucepan heat drippings. Sauté onions in drippings over medium heat until soft.

Add flour, salt, pepper, and garlic. Cook until brown.

Add parsley, thyme, stock, and wine. Simmer 45 minutes. Add cognac.

Toast 6 slices of French bread.

Make 3 "layers" in each bowl: toast, a sprinkle of cheese, and soup.

Top with more cheese and add a little melted butter.

Put under broiler until cheese forms crust.

Serves: 6

Potato Soup

6 slices bacon, cut into ½-inch pieces

2 cups onion, chopped

2 large leeks, white part only, sliced very thin

3 medium potatoes, peeled and cubed

1 large turnip, peeled and cubed

6 cups chicken broth

1 cup sour cream

Salt and pepper to taste

Snipped parsley for garnish

Fry bacon until crisp. Set aside.

Sauté onion and leeks in bacon fat until golden. Add potatoes, turnip, and chicken broth. Heat to boiling. Lower heat and simmer for 15 minutes or until potatoes and turnips are tender.

Purée in food processor or blender. Return to heat to keep warm.

Just before serving, stir in sour cream with wire whisk. Add salt and pepper to taste.

Garnish with bacon pieces and parsley. Serve immediately.

Serves: 8 to 10
Special Equipment: Food Processor/Blender

Sausage and Clam Stew

2 tablespoons olive oil

1 pound mushrooms, sliced

2 cups onions, sliced

1 pound hot Italian sausage
(casings removed) or ½ hot
and ½ mild

28-ounce can tomatoes
(undrained)

1 cup dry white wine

1 cup fresh or bottled clam juice

2 tablespoons fresh basil or 2
teaspoons dried

1 tablespoon garlic, minced

1 bunch parsley, chopped

2 pints chopped clams, fresh

In large Dutch oven, sauté mushrooms and onions separately in 1 tablespoon of olive oil each over medium heat.

Cook sausage and break up with fork. Stir frequently until sausage loses pink color, about 10 minutes. Drain sausage. Add onions and mushrooms. Stir in tomatoes. Bring mixture to boil, crushing tomatoes into small pieces.

Reduce heat to low and simmer for 5 minutes. Pour in wine and clam juice and return to boil. Reduce heat, cover, and simmer 20 minutes.

Add basil and garlic and cook 5 minutes longer. Add ½ of parsley (reserve the rest for garnish) and all the clams. Heat and serve.

Serves: 6 to 8
Special Equipment: Dutch oven

Italian Tortellini Soup

1 pound sweet Italian sausage, cut into ½-inch pieces

4 14-ounce cans beef broth

7 cups water

9-ounce box tortellini

9-ounce box spinach tortellini

½ pound cabbage, shredded

1 small green pepper, cored and diced

1 medium zucchini, sliced

1 small red onion, chopped

1 medium tomato, diced

1 tablespoon fresh basil, chopped

Salt and pepper

Freshly grated Parmesan cheese (optional)

Brown sausage. Combine everything but salt, pepper, and Parmesan in large pot. Season with salt and pepper. Bring to slow boil over medium-high heat.

Reduce heat and simmer until vegetables are tender, about 15 minutes.

Ladle soup into bowls. Serve immediately. Grated cheese may be served at the table.

Serves: 15

Vichyssoise

4 leeks
1 medium onion
2 tablespoons butter
5 medium potatoes, peeled and
    sliced into ¼-inch pieces
4 cups chicken stock
1 tablespoon salt
White pepper

2 cups milk
2 cups half and half
1 cup heavy cream
½ tablespoon sherry (optional)
¼ cup dry white wine (optional)
Chopped chives or cheddar
    cheese curls as garnish

Slice white part of leeks only. Slice onion. Sauté both in butter until golden.

Add potatoes, stock, salt, and pepper. Bring to a boil, simmer 35 to 40 minutes.

Process in blender until completely smooth, gradually adding milk and half and half.

Pour into large bowl and add heavy cream, sherry, and wine. Chill until very cold.

Garnish with chives or cheddar cheese curls.

Serves: 8 to 10
Special Equipment: Blender

Use milk to thin soup if necessary.

Tomato Consommé

4 cups chicken broth

16-ounce can plum tomatoes, finely chopped with juice

2 teaspoons tomato paste

½ teaspoon thyme

½ teaspoon basil

½ teaspoon allspice

2 teaspoons lemon juice

2 tablespoons dry sherry or Madeira

2 tablespoons chives or parsley, finely chopped

Place all ingredients except sherry or Madeira and chives or parsley in large sauce pan. Cook and stir until heated through.

Add wine just before serving. Garnish with chives or parsley.

Serves: 6

Purée of Yellow Squash Soup

2 pounds yellow squash, cut into chunks

½ cup chicken stock

1 ounce crystallized ginger

2½ cups heavy cream

3 tablespoons cognac

⅛ teaspoon ground mace

Salt and pepper to taste

Boil squash until tender (10 to 15 minutes). Drain well and pat dry. Purée with stock and ginger in blender until smooth.

Strain into a heavy saucepan. Stir in cream, cognac, mace, and salt and pepper to taste. Heat over medium heat and serve.

Serves: 6

Special Equipment: Blender

Cream of Zucchini Soup

¾ cup onion, chopped

2 tablespoons butter

1½ quarts chicken broth

5 cups zucchini, chopped

2 fresh basil leaves, chopped; or
¾ teaspoon dried

1 to 1½ cups heavy cream

Salt and pepper to taste

Shredded basil leaves or chopped chives; or dusting of nutmeg for garnish

Sauté onion in butter until transparent. Add chicken broth, zucchini, and basil. Simmer until tender, about 30 minutes.

Purée in food processor and return to pot. Add cream as desired (for a lower calorie version, use half milk and half cream).

Season with salt and pepper. Reheat gently to a simmer and serve garnished with basil, chives or nutmeg.

Serves: 8

Special Equipment: Food Processor

Very good served ice-cold and dusted with nutmeg.

Racing on the Long Island Sound

Salads, Dressings & Sauces

"The Toss"

Long Island justly deserves its reputation as "The Playground of New York." One thousand miles of shoreline are a magnet for millions of swimmers, sunbathers, sailors, and fishermen. We are blessed with more than 66,000 acres of parkland, offering sports enthusiasts a full range of amusements.

It is no surprise that our Island encourages water sports. By a recent count, our coastline supported 429 yacht clubs and marinas. Sailors compete heatedly in many local races, including the Around Long Island Regatta.

Sports on land are not neglected, however. Spectators can enjoy the world-famous U.S. Open at Flushing Meadows National Tennis Center each fall, or serve their own sets on one of hundreds of courts around the Island. Golfers tee up on 113 courses, including famous Shinnecock Hills, site of the 1987 U.S. Open Golf Championship.

Professional sports draw sell-out crowds on Long Island. Shea Stadium is the home of the New York Mets baseball team and the Islanders play ice hockey at Nassau Coliseum. Football's Jets practice and play pre-season games at Hofstra University. Thoroughbred racing had an early start on our Island at Belmont Park Race Track, which draws thousands during its annual season and for the running of the third leg of the coveted Triple Crown each spring. Horses also run for sport at Aqueduct Race Track. The Hamptons Classic Horse Show attracts equine fanciers to the East End each summer. Athletes who prefer to get around on their own two feet compete in the annual Long Island Marathon.

Chicken Salad Deluxe

2 cups cooked chicken, diced

1 14-ounce can artichoke hearts, drained and quartered

1 tablespoon chives, minced

½ teaspoon salt

Freshly ground pepper

½ cup ham, diced

1 tablespoon lemon juice

2 tablespoons salad oil

¾ cup mayonnaise

1 cup seedless grapes

Lettuce

¼ cup almonds, slivered

Cherry tomatoes, halved

Combine first six ingredients. Stir lemon juice and salad oil together and pour over chicken/artichoke mixture. Marinate in refrigerator 1 to 2 hours. When ready to serve, add grapes and toss with mayonnaise. Mound on lettuce leaves. Sprinkle with almonds. Garnish with cherry tomatoes.

Serves: 6

Macadamian Chicken Salad

1 teaspoon dry tarragon

2 tablespoons white wine

½ cup mayonnaise

½ cup sour cream

⅔ cup macadamia nuts, coarsely chopped

2 cups chicken breasts, poached and diced

Salt and pepper to taste

2 hard boiled eggs, peeled and sliced for garnishing

Capers for garnish

1 head Boston lettuce

Soak the tarragon in the white wine until soft, about ½ hour. Add mayonnaise and sour cream and mix thoroughly. Add nuts. Toss with chicken. Add salt and pepper to taste. Serve on lettuce and garnish with sliced eggs and capers.

Serves: 4 to 6

Cold Curried Chicken

3 pounds chicken cutlets
½ teaspoon onion salt
½ teaspoon celery salt
½ teaspoon nutmeg
½ teaspoon pepper
1 tablespoon olive oil
1 medium white onion, chopped
1 tablespoon curry

1 teaspoon chili sauce
Juice of half a lemon
2 tablespoons chutney
1¼ cups mayonnaise
2 tablespoons heavy cream
1½ cups uncooked rice
Parsley sprigs, paprika

Season chicken with onion salt, celery salt, nutmeg, and pepper. Bake at 350 degrees for 1 hour. Save stock and cool chicken.

Sauté onion in olive oil. Stir in curry. Add chicken stock, chili sauce, lemon juice, and chutney. Bring to a boil, then simmer 5 minutes.

Purée this mixture in blender and cool. Add mayonnaise and heavy cream. Refrigerate sauce until ready to serve.

Cook rice according to package directions, cool.

When ready to serve, start with a bed of greens, spoon rice into middle and arrange chicken around rice. Sprinkle with parsley and paprika. Pass with sauce.

Serves: 6 to 8

Curried Crab and Rice Salad

8 ounces crab meat, chopped
2 cups cooked rice, chilled
¼ cup green pepper, chopped
⅓ cup green onion, sliced
1 jar (6 ounce) marinated
   artichoke hearts

1 tablespoon curry powder
¼ cup mayonnaise
Salt and pepper to taste

Combine crab, rice, green peppers, and onions.

Drain artichoke hearts, reserve marinade. Cut hearts in half and add to crab mixture.

Mix 2 tablespoons of marinade with mayonnaise and curry powder. Pour over salad, toss, season and chill at least 1 hour.

Serves: 4 to 6

Terrific summer salad.

Vegetable Rice Salad

2 cups raw rice

4 cups chicken stock

¼ cup frozen peas, defrosted

¼ cup blanched almonds

¼ cup walnuts, chopped

¼ cup currants

¼ cup green pepper, chopped

¼ cup cucumber, chopped and seeded

French Dressing:

⅔ cup safflower oil

⅓ cup lemon juice

1 teaspoon Dijon mustard

Fresh dill to taste

2 cloves garlic, pressed

1 teaspoon chives

Cook rice in chicken stock until liquid is completely absorbed. Let cool a few minutes.

Combine rice with peas, almonds, walnuts, currants, pepper, and cucumber.

Whisk together oil and lemon juice. Add remaining ingredients. Pour over rice mixture and toss.

Serves: 6

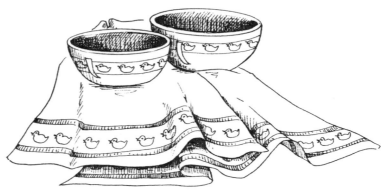

Ham and Endive Salad with Mustard Sauce

. . . .

1 pound boiled ham, thinly sliced
2 large heads Belgian endive
2 tablespoons Dijon mustard
1 tablespoon red wine vinegar
¼ teaspoon salt
Dash freshly ground pepper
¼ cup vegetable oil

1 tablespoon capers
1 tablespoon fresh parsley, chopped
1 tablespoon fresh chives, chopped
1 tablespoon onion, chopped
1 tablespoon fresh tarragon, (optional)

Stack ham slices on a flat surface, cut into ½-inch cubes. Put in a bowl.

Trim base off each endive. Pull off and save 10 or 12 of the best outside endive leaves to be used as garnish. Coarsely chop remaining endive. Add to ham.

Put mustard, vinegar, salt, and pepper in small bowl. Whisk in oil gradually, using a wire whisk. Stir in capers, parsley, chives, onion, and tarragon. Pour sauce over ham mixture and stir.

Line bowl with saved endive leaves, points up. Mound salad in center.

Serves: 6 to 8

Layered Broccoli Salad

1 head iceberg lettuce
1 cup celery, thinly sliced
½ red onion, thinly sliced
1¼ cups mayonnaise
1 tablespoon sugar

10 slices bacon, cooked and crumbled
1 cup mozzarella cheese, finely diced
1 package frozen broccoli, thawed but not cooked

Layer lettuce, celery, and onion in bowl.

Mix mayonnaise and sugar to create a dressing, and pour over lettuce. Top with cheese, broccoli, and bacon.

Toss just before serving.

Serves: 8 to 10

This is even better if made the day before and chilled overnight.

Salad Rose

1 head lettuce
1 cucumber, sliced
2 scallions, finely chopped
1 tin anchovies
3 hard-boiled eggs, quartered
1 large tomato, cut up

1 avocado, sliced
8 large raw mushrooms, sliced
6 ounces cooked chicken, finely chopped
6 ounces muenster cheese, finely cubed

Dressing:

½ cup olive oil
¼ cup balsamic vinegar
1 teaspoon Dijon mustard
1 small garlic clove, mashed

Juice of ½ lemon
¼ teaspoon salt
¼ teaspoon pepper
Parsley to garnish

Croutons:

6 slices white bread
½ cup olive oil
1 medium garlic clove

Salt and pepper to taste
Basil or oregano to taste

Wash and shred lettuce by hand. Place in large salad bowl. Arrange other ingredients attractively on lettuce.

Dressing: Mix dressing ingredients and pour over salad.

Croutons: Toast bread until dark. Allow to cool and harden in toaster. Rub garlic on both sides of toast; do not press or flavor will be too strong. Cut into cubes. Heat olive oil in frying pan. Place cubed bread into pan, sprinkle with salt, pepper, oregano, or basil leaves. Cook cubes over medium heat, stirring so they do not burn. Cool and sprinkle over salad.

Serves: 8

Copper Penny

. . . .

1½ pounds carrots
1 green pepper, diced
1 medium onion, diced
1 10-ounce can tomato soup
½ cup salad oil
½ cup cider vinegar

¼ cup sugar
1 teaspoon salt
1 teaspoon pepper
1 tablespoon Worcestershire
   sauce

Peel carrots and cut them into "coins" ⅛-inch thick. Bring a pot of salted water to a boil and cook carrots until nearly tender, about 6 minutes. They should retain a slight crunch. Drain. Add green pepper and onion to carrots.

Blend tomato soup, salad oil, cider vinegar, sugar, salt, pepper, and Worcestershire sauce and pour over carrots. Refrigerate until serving time.

Serves: 6 to 8

Summer Fresh Cucumber Salad

. . . .

4 firm cucumbers
1½ cups sour cream
1 small clove garlic, minced
2 tablespoon oil
2 teaspoon sugar

1 teaspoon salt
1 teaspoon white wine vinegar
½ teaspoon fresh dill, finely
   chopped

Peel cucumbers and slice thinly. Stir together remaining ingredients except dill. Pour over cucumbers and toss gently. Sprinkle with dill.

Cover and chill for at least 1 hour. May also be served at room temperature. Toss carefully before serving.

Serves: 10

. . . .

Green Beans with Tarragon

2 pounds green beans
3 cloves garlic
1 teaspoon salt
2 tablespoons vinegar
Dash of pepper
1 tablespoon mustard

6 tablespoons olive oil
3 tablespoons fresh tarragon or
   ½ teaspoon dried tarragon
½ cup fresh parsley
½ pound Gruyere, cubed

Cook green beans for 10 minutes. Drain and immediately run cold water over beans in colander. Chill beans until ready to use.

Put garlic and salt into bowl. Mash garlic and salt together, pour vinegar over salt and garlic mixture. Remove garlic. Add pepper, mustard and oil and whisk together. Set aside.

Chop parsley and tarragon together. Set aside.

When ready to serve, toss beans with dressing and put parsley, tarragon and Gruyere on top.

Serves: 8

Peas and Cheese Stuffed Tomatoes

2 cups cooked peas
1 cup cheddar cheese, cubed
2 hard boiled eggs, chopped
¼ cup celery
2 tablespoons onions, chopped
2 tablespoons pimento, chopped

⅓ cup mayonnaise
½ teaspoon salt
⅛ teaspoon pepper
¼ to ½ teaspoon Tabasco sauce
12 medium tomatoes
12 large lettuce leaves

In a large bowl, combine peas, cheese, eggs, celery, onions, and pimento.

In another bowl, combine mayonnaise, salt, pepper, and Tabasco sauce. Add to pea mixture and toss to coat.

Cover and chill several hours or overnight.

Cut each tomato into wedges, being careful not to cut all the way through. Spoon mixture on top and serve on lettuce leaves.

Serves: 12

Dilled Potato Salad

2 pounds red potatoes
½ cup sour cream
½ cup mayonnaise
2 green onions, minced, tops
   included
1½ teaspoons dried dill weed or
   1 tablespoon fresh dill

2 teaspoons Dijon mustard
1½ teaspoons lemon juice
Salt and pepper to taste
½ pound bacon, cooked and
   crumbled

Boil potatoes until tender, about 30 minutes. Rinse in cold water.

Cut potatoes in ½-inch cubes.

In large bowl combine sour cream, mayonnaise, onions, dill, mustard, lemon juice, salt, and pepper to taste.

Add cooked potatoes to dressing in bowl and toss to coat well.

Chill overnight.

Garnish with bacon just before serving.

Serves: 8

Dressing also makes a wonderful dip for vegetables.

Radish Salad

1 clove garlic, mashed
Salt to taste
2 tablespoons tarragon vinegar
6 tablespoons olive oil
1 tablespoon anchovy paste

1 teaspoon Dijon mustard
5 cups radishes, sliced
2 tablespoons scallions, minced
1 cup Gruyere, cubed

Garnish:
Black olives
Parsley, chopped

Rolled anchovy fillets

Mash garlic with salt; add vinegar. Remove garlic; add oil, anchovy paste, and mustard. Whisk.

Slice radishes in processor. Combine with scallions and Gruyere. Toss with dressing and chill.

When ready to serve, garnish with parsley, black olives and anchovies.

Serves: 8
Special Equipment: Food Processor

Ellen's Spinach and Cabbage Salad

1 pound spinach
1 red cabbage
¾ cup walnuts, chopped

⅓ cup raisins
½ red onion, sliced
1 teaspoon celery seed

Dressing:
⅔ cup vinegar
¾ cup sugar
2 teaspoons dry mustard

2 teaspoons salt
¼ cup onion, grated
2 cups vegetable oil

Thoroughly wash and dry spinach. Tear into small pieces. Shred cabbage. Add remaining ingredients.

Dressing: Combine dressing ingredients in blender or food processor. Add dressing to salad just before serving.

Serves: 8
Special Equipment: Food Processor / Blender

Bob's Caesar Salad

1 tablespoon salt
4 cloves garlic, peeled
2 tablespoons Dijon mustard
1 tablespoon fresh lemon juice
4 to 6 shakes Tabasco sauce
6 tablespoons olive oil

1 bunch Romaine lettuce
3 tablespoons Parmesan cheese
1 tablespoon garlic salt
1 can anchovies with liquid
1 egg, boiled 60 seconds
1 cup croutons

Sprinkle wooden bowl with salt.

Cut garlic cloves in half and rub the salt into the bowl.

Chop garlic and add mustard, lemon juice, Tabasco, and olive oil. Whisk mixture until salt dissolves and liquid blends.

Wash and dry lettuce, tear into bite-sized pieces and add to bowl.

Sprinkle with Parmesan cheese, garlic salt, add anchovies and break egg over salad.

Sprinkle with croutons and gently toss. Serve immediately.

Serves: 6
Special Equipment: Wooden bowl

Salade Orientale

Salad:

1½ pounds red peppers, seeded, cut diagonally, ¼ × 2-inch strips

2 bunches scallions, washed, dried, cut into thin diagonal slices

1¼ pounds fresh bean sprouts

1½ pounds Napa or Chinese cabbage, cut diagonally, 1 × 1½-inch strips

2½ pounds fresh spinach, washed, dried, and torn into bite-size pieces

Dressing:

1 cup vegetable oil

½ cup soy sauce

½ cup red wine vinegar

½ cup white sesame seeds, crushed in blender

1½ tablespoons fresh garlic, finely chopped

½ cup Hoisin sauce*

1 tablespoon fresh ginger, peeled and grated

Combine ingredients for dressing.

Combine salad ingredients and toss lightly with dressing.

Serves: 20

Special Equipment: Blender

This is an excellent buffet salad.

* available in gourmet or Oriental section of supermarket.

Tomato Mozzarella Cheese Toss

. . . .

4 to 6 ripe tomatoes, seeded and
  cut into 1-inch cubes
8 ounces mozzarella cheese, cut
  into ½-inch cubes

Freshly ground pepper to taste
1 cup pitted black olives, sliced

Dressing:
¼ cup fresh or ⅛ cup dried basil
4 tablespoons olive oil

1 to 2 tablespoons red wine
  vinegar

Combine all the salad ingredients. Prepare dressing, stirring well. Pour over salad. Serve well chilled.

Serves: 5 (Main) 10 (Buffet)

Beef and Mushroom Salad

. . . .

3 cups roast beef, sliced into
  1 × ½-inch strips
1 6-ounce can mushrooms, sliced
2½ tablespoons pimento,
  chopped

¼ cup Italian dressing
Lettuce

Slice beef into strips and put in bowl. Add mushrooms, pimentos, and salad dressing. Toss well. Refrigerate for several hours. Pass with slotted spoon (to drain some of dressing) and serve on bed of lettuce.

Serves: 6 to 8

This is excellent for beef leftovers.

. . . .

Zucchini Salad

¼ cup mayonnaise

¼ cup sour cream

1 tablespoon fresh lemon juice

1½ tablespoons Dijon mustard

4 cups zucchini, shredded and
 well drained

1¼ cups cherry tomatoes, halved

Bibb lettuce leaves

Watercress

In a small mixing bowl, combine mayonnaise, sour cream, lemon juice, and mustard thoroughly with a wire whisk. Chill covered for 1 hour (may be chilled for up to 4 hours).

When ready to serve, pour dressing over zucchini and tomatoes and toss lightly. Mound on a bed of lettuce leaves and watercress.

Serves: 4 to 6

Cold Sesame Noodles

. . . .

1 cup chicken, cooked and
   shredded

2 cups bean sprouts

1¼ pounds cappellini (or fine egg
   noodles)

2 tablespoons vegetable oil

1 tablespoon sesame oil

Peanuts, chopped (optional)

Sauce:

3 tablespoons tahini (sesame seed
   paste)

6 tablespoons soy sauce

1 tablespoon white vinegar

1 tablespoon chili oil

1 teaspoon sugar

2 tablespoons scallions, chopped

1½ teaspoons ground ginger

½ teaspoon freshly ground
   pepper

Bring large pot of water to boil. Put bean sprouts in a sieve, place into boiling water for 10 seconds. Rinse bean sprouts in cold water and drain.

Place noodles in boiling water. Cook according to package directions until tender. Drain.

Mix vegetable oil and sesame oil and toss with drained noodles. Cool.

Mix soy sauce into tahini one tablespoon at a time. Add remaining ingredients to make sauce.

To assemble: Layer in a large bowl: noodles, sprouts, chicken, sauce. Top with chopped peanuts if desired.

Serves: 8

This is for spicy food lovers.

. . . .

Pasta and Spinach Salad

½ pound thick sliced bacon, cut into 1-inch pieces

¼ cup butter

¾ cup sweet red pepper, diced

1 cup green onions, sliced

1 cup chicken broth

2 tablespoons lemon juice

Salt and pepper to taste

1 pound bow tie pasta

2 cups fresh mushrooms, sliced

10 ounces fresh spinach, well washed and torn into bite-sized pieces

1 cup Parmesan cheese

Cook bacon until crisp. Drain. Discard all but ¼ cup of bacon fat. Add butter to fat in skillet. Heat. Sauté onions and peppers until tender, about 2 minutes. Add chicken broth and lemon juice. Bring to a boil, lower heat and simmer 2 minutes. Add salt and pepper to taste. Remove sauce from heat.

Cook and drain pasta according to directions. Return to kettle. Add mushrooms and spinach. Add sauce and toss over moderate heat until sauce is absorbed and spinach is wilted. Divide among 4 heated plates. Top with grated cheese and bacon.

Serves: 4

A delicious and unusual luncheon dish.

Tortellini Salad

1 cup olive oil

½ cup balsamic vinegar

2 tablespoons Dijon mustard

2 cloves garlic, crushed

2 tablespoons fresh lemon juice

¼ teaspoon salt

¼ teaspoon freshly ground pepper

2 packages (15 ounce each) white tortellini with cheese

1 package (15 ounces) green tortellini with cheese

1 pound green beans, cut in 1-inch length

2 red bell peppers, cut in ¼-inch dice

1 bunch scallions (white and tender green), thinly sliced

1 cup fresh basil leaves, finely chopped

In large bowl, whisk together oil, vinegar, mustard, garlic, lemon juice, salt, and pepper.

In large pot of boiling, salted water, cook tortellini until tender, 10 to 12 minutes. Drain. Add tortellini to dressing and toss while pasta is hot.

In large saucepan of boiling, salted water, cook green beans until crisp and tender, 5 to 7 minutes. Drain and rinse under cold running water. Rinse again, thoroughly. Add peppers, scallions, and green beans to tortellini, toss well. Let cool to room temperature.

If making ahead, cover and refrigerate at this point. Return to room temperature 1 hour before serving. Just before serving, add the basil leaves and toss.

Serves: 18

Add a pint of cherry tomatoes and a can of artichoke hearts for additional color.

Poppy Seed and Honey Dressing

⅔ cup honey
Salt and pepper to taste
6 tablespoons prepared mustard

2 cups vegetable oil
1 small onion, minced
¾ tablespoon poppy seeds

Combine first five ingredients in blender or processor until thickened and oil disappears. Stir in poppy seeds.

Yield: 3 Cups
Special Equipment: Blender/Food Processor

Southern Salad Dressing

1 cup oil
⅓ cup red wine vinegar
2 cloves garlic, minced and mashed on back of spoon with ½ teaspoon salt
4 tablespoons sour cream

½ teaspoon dry mustard
1½ tablespoons sugar
2 teaspoons black pepper
3 teaspoons fresh parsley, chopped

Combine all ingredients in tightly covered jar or container. Store overnight in refrigerator. Shake well before serving.

Yield: 1½ Cups

For best results, should be made ahead.

Blue Cheese Dressing

1 cup buttermilk
1 cup mayonnaise
1 teaspoon vinegar

1 teaspoon garlic powder, or to taste
4 ounces blue cheese

Blend all ingredients together being careful not to over process.

Yield: 3 Cups
Special Equipment: Blender

An easy gourmet touch to a simple salad.

Dijon Vinaigrette

6 tablespoons olive oil
2 tablespoons red wine vinegar
1 teaspoon Dijon mustard

1 teaspoon lemon juice
1 teaspoon salt
Freshly ground pepper to taste

Combine all ingredients in tightly covered jar or container and shake. Shake again before using.

Yield: ½ Cup

Double or triple this to always have some on hand.

Tangy Lime Dressing

¾ cup olive oil
⅓ cup fresh lime juice
2 teaspoons Tabasco sauce
½ to 1 teaspoon ground cumin
¼ teaspoon black pepper

Salt to taste
Pinch of sugar
Fresh pineapple, sliced
Mandarin oranges
Lettuce

Combine first seven ingredients in a tightly covered jar and shake. Refrigerate. Shake before serving. Serve over fresh sliced pineapple and mandarin oranges on a bed of lettuce.

Yield: 1 Cup

Therese's Vinaigrette

2 tablespoons Dijon mustard
1 teaspoon garlic salt
½ teaspoon ground pepper

2 tablespoons wine vinegar
6 tablespoons vegetable oil

Mix all the ingredients together several hours before using. Refrigerate. Serve over mixed greens.

Yield: ½ Cup

Keeps in refrigerator for several weeks.

Horseradish Mousse

½ cup whipping cream
3 tablespoons well drained
prepared horseradish

2 teaspoons onion, grated
¼ teaspoon salt
1 teaspoon lemon juice

Whip cream and gently fold in horseradish, salt, onion, and lemon juice.

Chill.

Yield: 1 Cup

Excellent as accompaniment to rib roast.

Lemon Butter Sauce

¼ cup butter
1 tablespoon fresh lemon juice
1 tablespoon fresh parsley,
chopped

Dash pepper
Dash cayenne

Melt butter by microwaving 30 seconds to 1 minute on high setting.

Add lemon juice, parsley, pepper, and cayenne.

Serve immediately over fish or chicken.

Yield: ¼ Cup
Special Equipment: Microwave

Long Island White Clam Sauce

Olive oil

5 cloves garlic, peeled and crushed

2 dried red peppers or 2 teaspoons red pepper flakes

2 8-ounce bottles clam juice

3 to 4 dozen raw clams, chopped plus their juice

1 bunch Italian parsley, chopped

Coat bottom of sauce pan with olive oil.

Sauté garlic cloves and inside seeds of red pepper until golden brown. Discard garlic.

Add bottled clam juice, raw clams and Italian parsley. Warm over low heat approximately 10 to 15 minutes (do not boil).

Serve over fresh linguine.

Yield: 4 Cups

Marinara Sauce

½ cup olive oil

4 cloves garlic, peeled and minced

1 teaspoon dried oregano

16 ounce can crushed tomatoes with tomato purée

1 teaspoon dried basil

1 teaspoon Italian parsley, finely chopped

Salt and pepper to taste

1 teaspoon crushed red pepper (optional)

Heat oil in saucepan. Add garlic, oregano, and pepper (be careful not to let garlic burn). Add tomatoes. Stir. Add basil and parsley. Add salt and pepper to taste. Simmer for 30 minutes. Serve on pasta.

Yield: 2½ Cups

Marmalade Sauce For Chicken

1 cup sweet orange marmalade

1 8-ounce can tomato sauce

2 tablespoons onion, chopped

1½ teaspoons soy sauce

1 teaspoon ground ginger

½ cup almonds, sliced

Combine all ingredients in a 1½ quart casserole dish.

Microwave on high for 5 to 7 minutes, stirring every 2 minutes until hot. May also be done on stove over low heat.

Yield: 2 Cups
Special Equipment: Microwave

Patty's Mustard Sauce

1 cup malt vinegar
2 2-ounce boxes dry mustard

3 eggs, beaten
1 cup sugar

Combine vinegar and mustard. Chill overnight.

Combine with beaten eggs and sugar in double boiler.

Heat over simmering water, stirring with a whisk for 7 minutes.

Store in refrigerator.

Yield: 2½ Cups
Special Equipment: Double boiler

Put this into a pretty jar and give as a hostess gift.

Spiked Barbecue Sauce

½ cup Hoisin paste (or thickest
   jar version available)
1 cup honey
½ cup bourbon

1 cup tomato purée
1 clove garlic, peeled and minced
1 teaspoon soy sauce

Combine all ingredients. Brush sauce on chicken or lamb.

Yield: 3 Cups

Even better after a few days in the refrigerator!

Spicy Mustard Sauce

½ cup dry mustard

¼ cup mustard seed

½ cup cider vinegar

⅓ cup white wine vinegar

3 tablespoons honey

2 tablespoons horseradish, drained

1 teaspoon red pepper flakes

Combine all ingredients in blender until smooth.

Yield: 1 Cup
Special Equipment: Blender

Makes an excellent barbeque sauce or marinade for beef or chicken.

Too Easy To Be True Barbecue Sauce

1 cup ketchup

½ cup soy sauce

1 teaspoon garlic powder

Mix ingredients together and spread on chicken or ribs.

Yield: 1½ Cups

So much better than store bought!

Roosevelt Summer White House — Sagamore Hill

Breads, Muffins & Beverages

"The Slice"

Walt Whitman, Fanny Brice, Andy Warhol . . . a most unlikely trio. Nevertheless, they shared a love for Long Island, which has been home or refuge for famous folks throughout the years. Peaceful country settings within easy traveling distance of the cultural and economic giant, Manhattan, have always made Long Island a desirable retreat.

A few of the writers in addition to Whitman who found peace and inspiration here include William Cullen Bryant, Arthur Miller, James Fenimore Cooper, John Steinbeck, Norman Mailer, Truman Capote, and John Updike. Musicians as varied as Harry Chapin, Eddie Cantor, Paul Simon, Al Jolson, and Billy Joel were born or have had homes on the Island.

The resort areas of the East End and Hamptons appeal to such popular figures as Alan Alda, Kathleen Turner, Chevy Chase, Ralph Lauren, and Charlotte Ford. Former screen and stage greats such as Fanny Brice and Nicky Arnstein, Ed Wynn, Groucho Marx, Basil Rathbone, and Lillian Russell also lived here for a time. Various Roosevelts, Vanderbilts, and Kennedys still relax in Island homes.

The light, the lifestyle, and the proximity to New York have attracted artists to the Island for years. Nineteenth century painters who found inspiration on Long Island include William Sidney Mount, Winslow Homer, and Thomas Moran. Some of the contemporary artists who value the "isolated splendor" of the South Shore and the East End are George Luks, Maurice Prendergast, Jackson Pollock, Willem deKooning, Charles Addams, Saul Steinberg, Roy Lichtenstein, and Robert Rauschenberg.

Apple Breakfast Bread

1 cup shortening
2 cups sugar
2 eggs
½ teaspoon cinnamon
½ teaspoon nutmeg
1 teaspoon salt

1 teaspoon baking soda
2 teaspoons vanilla
3 cups flour
3 cups unpeeled apples, diced
1 cup walnuts, chopped
  (optional)

Mix shortening, sugar, eggs, cinnamon, nutmeg, salt, baking soda, and vanilla in a bowl.

Add flour, diced apples, and nuts. Stir. (Mixture will be very thick.)

In ungreased tube pan or 2 ungreased loaf pans, bake at 325 degrees for 90 minutes.

Let cool 30 minutes. Remove from pan and serve warm.

Yield: 2 loaves
Special Equipment: Tube pan/2 loaf pans

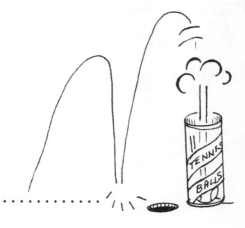

Nan's Banana Bread

1 cup sugar
½ cup butter or margarine, softened
2 medium or large eggs
2 cups flour

Dash salt
1 teaspoon baking soda dissolved in ⅓ cup hot water
3 ripe bananas
½ cup walnuts, chopped

Cream sugar, butter, and eggs together. Blend in flour and salt.

Add dissolved baking soda and bananas, and mix well with electric mixer. Fold in nuts.

In loaf pan, bake at 350 degrees for 1 hour. Test doneness with knife.

Yield: 1 loaf

Beer Bread

3 cups self-rising flour
3 tablespoons sugar

1 egg
12 ounces beer

Mix all ingredients in bowl. Let rise 5 minutes. Bake in greased loaf pan at 375 degrees for 35 to 40 minutes.

Yield: 1 loaf

This is especially good served with cheese.

Orange Pecan Bread

½ cup sweet butter, softened
¾ cup sugar
2 eggs, separated
Grated rind of 1 large orange
1½ cups flour

1½ teaspoons baking powder
¼ teaspoon baking soda
Pinch of salt
½ cup fresh orange juice
1 cup shelled pecans, chopped

Glaze:

¼ cup fresh orange juice

¼ cup sugar

Preheat oven to 350 degrees. Grease three mini loaf pans.

Cream butter. Add sugar to butter gradually, beating with electric mixer until light. Beat in egg yolks one at time. Add orange rind.

Sift together flour, baking powder, baking soda, salt, and add to batter alternately with orange juice, beginning and ending with flour. Gently fold in pecans.

Beat egg whites until stiff, and fold carefully into batter. Pour into greased pans and bake for 30 minutes.

For glaze, boil orange juice and sugar for 3 minutes and pour over cooled loaves.

Yield: 3 small loaves
Special Equipment: 3 mini loaf pans

Excellent for holiday gift-giving.

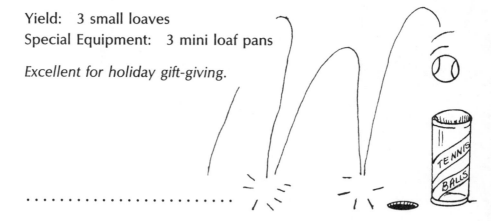

Oregano Parmesan Bread

1 cup milk
1 cup water
2 tablespoons dry yeast
2 tablespoons butter, softened

2 tablespoons salt
½ tablespoon oregano
½ cup Parmesan cheese, grated
4½ cups flour

Heat milk and water until lukewarm.

Add all ingredients except 1¼ cups flour and 1 tablespoon cheese.

Mix with electric mixer. Fold in remaining flour. Cover with wax paper and paper towel and let dough rise in a warm place for 45 minutes.

Knead and shape into loaf and put in greased loaf pan.

Sprinkle with remaining cheese and bake at 400 degrees for 55 minutes.

Yield: 1 loaf

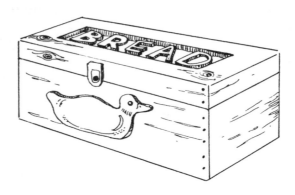

Staff of Life Bread

2 packages yeast
½ cup warm water
1 cup bran cereal
1 cup oatmeal
2 tablespoons oil
1 tablespoon salt

2¾ cups boiling water
⅓ cup honey
⅓ cup molasses
1 cup stone-ground whole wheat flour
6 cups white flour

Mix yeast in ½ cup warm water. Set aside.

In large bowl, combine bran, oatmeal, oil, salt, and boiling water. Let cool, then add yeast.

Add honey, molasses, whole wheat flour, and white flour. Mix with a heavy duty mixer.

Place in bowl and let rise until double in bulk. Punch down. Let rise again in bread pans. (You can hasten rising action by covering dough with cloth and placing in warm oven.)

Bake at 350 degrees for 55 minutes.

Yield: 2 loaves
Special Equipment: Heavy duty mixer

Great with a hearty soup for a winter meal.

Tomato Soup Walnut Bread

2 cups flour
1 tablespoon baking powder
½ teaspoon baking soda
½ teaspoon cloves
½ teaspoon cinnamon
½ teaspoon nutmeg

1 cup walnuts, coarsely chopped
½ cup butter
1 cup sugar
2 eggs, well beaten
10-ounce can condensed tomato soup

Sift together first 6 ingredients.

Stir in walnuts. Set dry ingredient mixture aside.

Cream butter. Stir sugar into butter gradually until fluffy. Add eggs and beat well.

Add ⅓ dry ingredients, then ½ can soup. Repeat, ending with dry ingredients. Beat only enough to blend after each addition.

Pour into well-greased 9×5-inch loaf pan. Bake for 1 hour at 350 degrees. Cool in pan on wire rack 10 minutes before removing from pan. Cool thoroughly before slicing.

Yield: 1 loaf

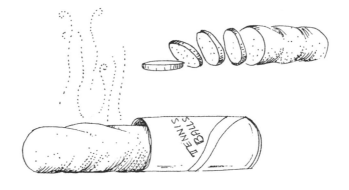

Swedish Orange Rye Bread

1 package yeast	Grated rind of 2 oranges
Water	¾ teaspoon salt
⅓ cup sugar	2½ cups unsifted rye flour
¼ cup molasses	2½ cups unsifted all-purpose
2 tablespoons shortening	flour

Sprinkle yeast into ¼ cup lukewarm water, stir until dissolved.

Combine 1½ cups lukewarm water, sugar, molasses, shortening, orange rind, salt, and yeast mixture in large bowl. Add flours gradually, beating until smooth.

Knead dough lightly on lightly floured board. Turn into greased bowl. Cover.

Let rise in a warm place until nearly doubled in bulk. Punch down, shape into 2 loaves. Place loaves in greased 9×5×3-inch loaf pans.

Let rise again until almost doubled. Bake at 375 degrees for 40 minutes.

Yield: 2 loaves

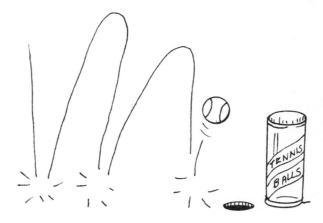

Cranberry Nut Coffee Cake

¼ cup brown sugar
⅓ cup walnuts, chopped
½ teaspoon cinnamon
2 cups Bisquick

2 tablespoons sugar
1 egg
⅔ cup water
⅔ cup whole cranberry sauce

Icing:

1 cup confectioners sugar
½ teaspoon vanilla

1 tablespoon water or more as needed

Preheat oven to 400 degrees. Grease 9×9×2-inch pan.

Mix brown sugar, nuts, and cinnamon in small bowl and set aside.

Combine Bisquick, sugar, egg, and water. Beat vigorously for 1 minute or until most lumps are gone.

Spread into pan. Sprinkle with nut mixture. Spoon cranberry sauce on top.

Bake for 20 to 25 minutes.

To make icing, mix confectioners sugar, vanilla, and water for about 1 minute until smooth. While cake is still warm, spread icing over top.

Serves: 4 to 6

Zucchini Nut Bread

3 cups zucchini, grated and well-drained

3 large eggs

2 cups sugar

3 cups flour

1 cup salad oil

1 teaspoon salt

3 teaspoons cinnamon

1½ cups walnuts, ground (optional)

¾ cup raisins (optional)

2 teaspoons vanilla

1 teaspoon baking soda

1 teaspoon baking powder

Preheat oven to 350 degrees. Grease two 9-inch loaf pans.

In large mixing bowl beat eggs. Add sugar and mix well. Add zucchini, flour, oil, salt, cinnamon, walnuts, raisins, vanilla, baking soda, and baking powder. Mix well.

Pour into greased loaf pans and bake at 350 degrees for 1 hour.

Yield: 2 loaves

Out East Oatmeal Pancakes

2½ cups sifted flour

2 tablespoons sugar

1 teaspoon baking powder

1 teaspoon baking soda

1 teaspoon salt

½ cup oatmeal

2 eggs

2 cups buttermilk

5 tablespoons butter, melted, or corn oil

Sift flour, sugar, baking powder, baking soda, and salt together. Stir in oatmeal. Add eggs, buttermilk, and melted butter. Drop onto hot griddle in desired sizes.

Cook on one side until bubbles appear and top looks dry. Flip pancakes and cook until bottom is browned.

Serves: 4 to 6

French Bread Toast

6 eggs
1½ cups milk
3 tablespoons granulated sugar
1½ teaspoons vanilla

⅜ teaspoon nutmeg
1 loaf French bread, cut into
 ¾-inch slices
½ cup butter, melted

Beat eggs. Stir in milk. Add sugar, vanilla, and nutmeg. Stir well.

Place bread slices on rimmed baking sheet. Pour mixture over the bread. Let stand a few minutes then turn over. When entire mixture has been absorbed, freeze in pan.

Preheat oven to 375 degrees. Take pan from freezer and release frozen slices by dipping bottom of baking sheet into hot water.

Brush butter on both sides of bread and place on clean cookie sheet. Bake at 375 degrees for 10 minutes on one side. Turn over and bake 8 minutes longer.

Serve immediately with your best maple syrup.

Serves: 6

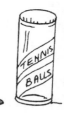

Blueberry Muffins

1½ cups fresh blueberries
¼ cup sweet butter
½ cup granulated sugar
1 egg
2¼ cups all-purpose flour

4 teaspoons baking powder
½ teaspoon salt
¼ teaspoon cinnamon
1 cup milk
1 teaspoon vanilla

Topping:
½ teaspoon cinnamon
⅓ cup flour

¼ cup cold sweet butter
½ cup sugar

Place blueberries into colander and wash gently. Spread blueberries on paper towels and pat dry.

In mixing bowl, cream butter and sugar until fluffy. Beat in egg.

Mix together flour, baking powder, salt, and cinnamon. Add dry ingredients to sugar and egg mixture alternately with milk, beginning and ending with the flour mixture.

Add vanilla and mix well. Gently fold in blueberries. Spoon evenly into 12 buttered muffin tins.

Mix together cinnamon, flour, butter, and sugar until crumbly. Sprinkle over muffins.

Bake at 375 degrees for 25 minutes or until golden brown.

Yield: 12 muffins

Bran Muffins

3 cups bran cereal
1 cup boiling water
½ cup melted shortening
1½ cups sugar
2 eggs, beaten

2 cups buttermilk
2½ cups flour
2½ teaspoons baking soda
1 teaspoon salt

Can also add:
¼ cup dates, raisins, or chopped
  apple

Pour boiling water over 1 cup of bran and let stand for 10 minutes while following steps 2 and 3.

Mix rest of bran with shortening, sugar, eggs, and buttermilk.

Sift flour with soda and salt.

Combine all ingredients. Fill muffin tins ⅔ full and bake at 400 degrees for 20 minutes.

Yield: 2½ to 3 dozen muffins

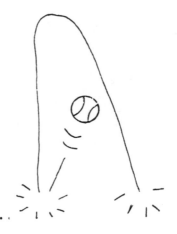

Orange Muffins

1 cup butter
1 cup sugar
2 eggs
1 teaspoon baking soda
2 cups flour

1 cup buttermilk
Grated rind of 2 oranges
½ cup pecans, chopped
1 cup brown sugar
Juice of 2 oranges

Cream together butter and sugar. Add eggs and mix.

Mix together baking soda and flour and add to sugar mixture, alternating with buttermilk. Stir grated rind and pecans into batter.

Fill greased muffin tins and bake for 20 minutes at 400 degrees, or until golden brown. Check after 15 minutes.

Mix brown sugar with orange juice. Pour mixture over hot muffins in tins and remove muffins immediately.

Yield: 24 regular muffins

Pumpkin Muffins

1 cup white flour
½ cup whole wheat flour
½ cup sugar
2 teaspoons baking powder
1¼ teaspoons cinnamon
½ teaspoon ground ginger
¼ teaspoon ground cloves
½ cup golden raisins

1 egg, slightly beaten
½ cup lowfat milk
¾ cup canned solid-pack pumpkin
¼ cup butter or margarine, melted
1 teaspoon cinnamon and 1 teaspoon sugar, mixed together

Sift together flours, sugar, baking powder, cinnamon, ginger, and cloves into bowl. Add raisins.

Combine egg, milk, pumpkin, and butter.

Add wet ingredients to dry ingredients all at once, stirring only until combined. Do not beat.

Pour batter into muffin tins lined with paper or foil liners. Sprinkle cinnamon sugar mixture on top.

Bake at 400 degrees for about 25 minutes.

Yield: 1 dozen muffins

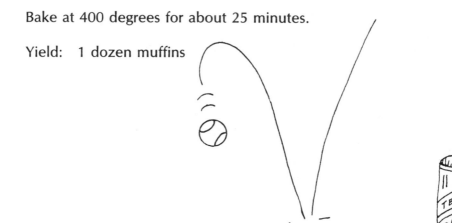

Tavern Sweet Potato Muffins

½ cup butter
½ cup white sugar
½ cup brown sugar
2 eggs
1¼ cups canned sweet potatoes, mashed
1½ cups flour
2 teaspoons baking powder

¼ teaspoon salt
1 teaspoon cinnamon
¼ teaspoon nutmeg
1 cup milk
¼ cup nuts (walnuts or pecans), chopped
½ cup raisins, chopped

Grease muffin tins.

Cream butter and sugars. Add eggs and mix well. Blend in sweet potatoes.

Sift flour with baking powder, salt, cinnamon, and nutmeg. Add flour mixture to sweet potatoes alternately with milk. Do not overmix. Fold in nuts and raisins.

Fill tins ⅔ full. Bake at 400 degrees for 25 minutes.

Yield: 2 to 3 dozen muffins

These muffins are perfect with Virginia ham dinner.

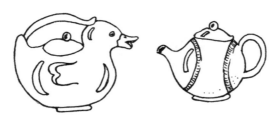

Peach Punch

1 cup peaches, sliced
1 cup peach schnapps

2 bottles champagne

Put peach slices into a pitcher. Pour in schnapps and let peaches marinate for half an hour.

When ready to serve, slowly add champagne to schnapps. Place a peach slice in each glass before adding punch.

Serves: 8 to 10

Russian Tea

2 cups powdered orange drink
1 envelope lemonade mix,
   unsweetened
½ cup sugar

½ cup instant tea
1 teaspoon cinnamon
½ teaspoon cloves
½ teaspoon nutmeg

Mix all ingredients well. Use 2 heaping teaspoons to a cup of boiling water or to 8 ounces of cold water.

Yield: 4 gallons

Block Island

. . . .

1 jigger (1 ounce) good rum　　　　**Slice of lime**
1 bottle Orangina

Pour jigger of rum into highball glass.

Fill glass ¾ full with Orangina.

Add crushed ice.

Add slice of lime.

Serves:　1

Orange Mint Cooler

. . . .

6-ounce can frozen orange juice　　**1 tray ice cubes**
6 ounces water　　　　　　　　　　**⅛ cup sugar**
6 ounces milk　　　　　　　　　　　**4 to 6 large sprigs fresh mint**
Dash vanilla

Blend first 6 ingredients in a blender, pour into a goblet, and add a generous sprig of mint.

Serves:　6 to 8
Special Equipment:　Blender

. . . .

Mock Cappuccino

1 quart half and half
2 cups strong coffee
¼ cup honey
1½ tablespoons cocoa,
    unsweetened
1 tablespoon vanilla
¾ cup cognac or brandy

½ cup plus 2 tablespoons coffee
    liqueur
½ cup rum
1 tablespoon Galliano
Whipped cream
Shaved semi-sweet chocolate

In large saucepan, combine half and half, coffee, honey, cocoa, and vanilla.

Cook over medium heat, stirring until almost scalded.

Remove from heat and stir in cognac, coffee liqueur, rum, and Galliano.

Pour into heated mugs or cups.

Top with whipped cream and garnish with shaved chocolate.

Yield: 12 Cups

Holiday Glogg

1 gallon claret or hearty
   burgundy wine
1 pound brown sugar
1 cup dark seedless raisins
1 cup dried apricots

1 cup almonds, shelled
4 whole cinnamon sticks
1 pint brandy
1 heaping teaspoon whole cloves
   tied up in cheese cloth

Place all ingredients into large pot and stir briefly. Heat over low flame and simmer for at least 3 hours. Remove cloves before serving.

Keeps for at least 2 weeks unrefrigerated. Reheat before serving.

Yield: 1 Gallon

Improves with age.

Wassail

2 quarts sweet apple cider
2 cups orange juice
1 cup lemon juice
1 cup pineapple juice

1 stick whole cinnamon
1 teaspoon whole cloves
Honey

Combine all ingredients in large saucepan. Sweeten to taste with honey. Simmer and strain.

Yield: 3 quarts

Especially nice at holiday time.

South Shore Fishing Boats at Dock

Entrées

"On Centre Court"

The first Island residents, the Indians, supported their peaceful lifestyle with the produce of the sea. Today, the ocean continues to be generous to Long Island. More than 10,000 full and part-time commercial fishermen reel in thirty-six million pounds of fish annually, grossing an estimated forty-five million dollars. Flounder is the most profitable catch, but porgies, bluefish, Atlantic mackerel, bass, and whiting also abound.

The flotillas of sport fishermen are hardly left adrift. More than one-third of all the fish caught in Long Island waters is hooked by sportsmen fishing from boats, piers, or surf. Giant tuna weighing up to 1,000 pounds are avidly sought by amateur and commercial fishermen alike and just as avidly snapped up at the Montauk docks, to be air-freighted within hours to sushi lovers from Tokyo to San Francisco.

Shell fishing has provided food and employment for centuries. Gourmets can savour oysters from famous Blue Point and Oyster Bay, as well as mussels and lobsters from Long Island Sound. The fall harvest of flavorful Peconic Bay scallops has declined significantly in the past decade but the tiny morsels continue to grace Island tables, mostly during the harvest season. The Great South Bay and other Long Island waters produce more hard-shell clams for market than any other area of the United States.

Flank Steak Roulade

3 or 4 large whole scallions
1½ pounds flank steak, well
   trimmed

Marinade:

½ cup soy sauce

1 clove garlic, chopped

¼ cup white wine

½ teaspoon ginger, minced

2 tablespoons sesame oil

1 teaspoon sugar

Place scallions lengthwise on steak. Roll steak, jelly roll fashion, secure with twine.

Combine all ingredients for marinade and pour over steak. Allow steak to marinate in refrigerator for a minimum of 3 hours.

Remove from marinade and grill for 10 to 15 minutes, turning steak frequently.

Periodically check for desired doneness. Slice into rounds.

Serves: 4 to 6
Special Equipment: Grill

A favorite with all members of the family!

Anne Marie's Beef Wellington

1 3-pound filet of beef
2 tablespoons butter, melted

Salt and pepper

Filling:
1 tablespoon butter
1 medium onion, finely chopped
½ pound good quality liverwurst

¼ cup heavy cream
4 tablespoons cognac
1 black truffle, sliced (optional)

Pastry:
3 cups all-purpose flour
1 teaspoon salt
½ cup butter
¼ cup shortening

1 egg yolk
¼ cup ice water
1 egg, beaten

Preheat oven to 450 degrees.

Brush melted butter over filet and sprinkle with salt and pepper. Place uncovered in roasting pan and cook for 15 minutes for rare, 20 to 25 minutes for medium. Remove from oven and allow to cool completely.

Heat 1 tablespoon of butter in small skillet and sauté onion. Remove casing from liverwurst. Place in bowl with onion, cream, and cognac. Mix well. Spread pâté evenly on top and sides of filet. If using truffle, press slices on top of pâté.

In a medium bowl, combine flour and salt. Add butter and shortening and combine with pastry blender. Add egg yolk and water, one tablespoon at a time, until a dough is formed. Cover with plastic wrap and chill.

Continued on next page

Reheat oven to 425 degrees.

Roll out dough to a 12×18-inch rectangle, saving scraps. Place filet, top side down, on center of dough. Bring up sides and ends around filet and brush seam with beaten egg.

Turn upside down and transfer to lightly greased baking pan and brush completely with beaten egg. Cut out decorative shapes from pastry trimmings, arrange on top of pastry and brush with egg.

Bake for 20 to 30 minutes or until pastry is light brown.

Serves: 12

Beef Tenderloin with Sauce Poivre Vert

. . . .

1 beef tenderloin (5 to 5½ pounds), fully trimmed

2 tablespoons butter

3 slices bacon

Marinade:

1 cup dry white wine

¼ cup brandy

2 tablespoons oil

1 teaspoon salt

6 black peppercorns

1 clove garlic, minced

1 bay leaf

½ teaspoon dried tarragon

Sauce Poivre Vert:

½ cup onion, finely minced

1 cup reserved marinade

2 tablespoons green peppercorns, rinsed and drained

1 cup heavy cream

1 tablespoon Dijon mustard

1 teaspoon salt

Combine all marinade ingredients in a stainless steel or enamel bowl. Add meat, turn to distribute marinade, and refrigerate. Marinate at least 8 hours, turning several times.

Preheat oven to 400 degrees. Drain meat and reserve marinade. Rub meat with butter, lay slices of bacon on top, and place meat on a rack in an oiled roasting pan.

Roast in middle of oven, basting occasionally, for about 45 minutes or until meat thermometer reaches 125 degrees.

Continued on next page

. . . .

Continued *Beef Tenderloin with Sauce Poivre Vert*

Remove from oven, cover with tent of foil, and allow to stand 15 or 20 minutes while you make sauce.

Sauce: Pour off all but 3 tablespoons of accumulated fat from roasting pan.

Place pan over heat; add onions and cook until soft. Add reserved marinade and stir to release browned particles in pan.

Reserve 1 teaspoon peppercorns and crush rest. Stir peppercorns in pan with cream, mustard, and salt to taste. Boil sauce to thicken about 3 or 4 minutes. Stir in rest of peppercorns. Slice meat and serve with sauce on the side.

Serves: 10 to 12
Special Equipment: Meat thermometer

Spicy New England Pot Roast

3 tablespoons flour

2 teaspoons salt

¼ teaspoon black pepper, freshly ground

4-pound bottom round pot roast of beef

3 tablespoons bacon drippings or oil

4-ounce jar horseradish sauce

1 can cranberry sauce, whole berry or sauce

1 stick cinnamon, broken in two

6 whole cloves

1 can beef broth or 4 bouillon cubes with 1 cup water

10 whole black peppercorns

2 bay leaves

Cornstarch

Mix flour with salt and pepper and dredge meat in mixture. Rub mixture into all surfaces.

Heat bacon drippings or oil in heavy dutch oven and brown meat on all sides over very high heat until it is well seared. Pour off oil.

Mix together horseradish, cranberry sauce, cinnamon, cloves, broth, peppercorns, and bay leaves. Add to meat.

Bring mixture to a boil, cover, and simmer gently for 2 to 3 hours. At end of cooking time, set aside meat. Strain gravy. Thicken with cornstarch if desired.

Serves: 6 to 8
Special Equipment: Dutch oven

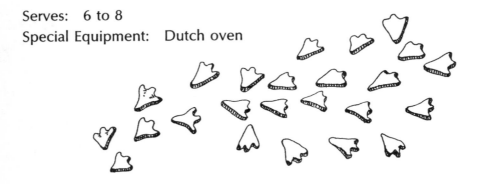

Scrumptious Chili

1½ pounds ground chuck
¼ cup flour
3 to 4 tablespoons chili powder
1 to 2 tablespoons cumin
2 medium onions, peeled
1 green pepper, seeded

2 cloves garlic, peeled
1 large can (32-ounce) crushed tomatoes
2 small (16-ounce) cans kidney beans or pork and beans with liquid
Cheddar cheese, grated

Brown meat until it loses its pink color. Add flour and stir until all grease is absorbed. Add chili and cumin and stir.

Grind onion, garlic, and green pepper together in food processor and add to meat with any juice that is created.

Add tomatoes and beans. Simmer uncovered on low heat at least 3 hours.

Sprinkle with grated cheddar cheese before serving.

Serves: 8 to 10
Special Equipment: Food Processor/Blender

Boeuf a la Bourguignonne

. . . .

1½ pound piece lean bacon trimmed of rind and cut in 1 x ¼ x ¼ inch strips (or ½ pound sliced lean bacon cut up)

1 quart water

4 pounds boned beef chuck or rump cut into 1½ inch cubes

1 tablespoon olive oil

2 carrots, peeled, sliced thin

2 medium-sized yellow onions, sliced thin

3 tablespoons flour

1 teaspoon salt (optional)

¼ teaspoon pepper

1 bottle (750 ml) dry red wine

3 (10½ ounce) cans condensed beef broth

2 cloves garlic, peeled and crushed

2 4-inch sprigs fresh thyme or ½ teaspoon dried thyme

1 bay leaf

1 pound mushrooms

2 tablespoons butter or margarine

Simmer bacon in water uncovered for 10 minutes. Drain, pat dry, and brown in large heavy kettle over moderately high heat 5 minutes. Drain on paper towel. Brown meat in bacon drippings a few pieces at a time and drain on paper towel.

Add oil to kettle. Reduce heat to moderate. Add carrots and onions and stir-fry 8 to 10 minutes until golden. Return beef and bacon to kettle. Add flour, seasonings and toss to mix. Add wine, broth, garlic, thyme and bay leaf, cover and simmer, stirring occasionally 1½ to 2 hours until beef is tender. Sauté mushrooms in butter until golden. Set aside.

When beef is tender, remove thyme sprigs if used, add mushrooms and simmer 10 to 15 minutes longer. If stew seems thick, add 1 cup boiling water.

Serves: 8

. . . .

Herbed Veal with Lemon

8 1½-ounce veal scallops
Salt and freshly ground pepper
½ cup all-purpose flour
¼ cup (½ stick) butter
1 tablespoon olive oil
2 tablespoons dry white wine
½ cup chicken broth

2 tablespoons fresh lemon juice
2 tablespoons green onion, finely chopped
1 tablespoon minced fresh parsley
½ teaspoon rosemary
Freshly cooked rice or pasta

Season veal with salt and pepper. Dredge veal in flour to coat, shaking off excess.

Melt butter with oil over medium-high heat until hot, but not brown. Add veal and sauté quickly on both sides, turning frequently. Transfer veal to heated platter.

Pour wine into skillet and stir, scraping up any browned bits. Blend in broth, lemon juice, onion, parsley, and rosemary. Reduce heat, cover, and simmer gently, stirring frequently for 3 to 5 minutes.

Return veal to skillet. Simmer gently until tender 1 to 2 minutes. Spoon over rice or pasta. Serve immediately.

Serves: 4

Mushrooms and Veal Scallops

6 veal cutlets, about 2 pounds
5 tablespoons butter
¼ cup olive oil
2 tablespoons shallots, chopped
¼ cup dry white wine

⅓ cup chicken broth
½ cup heavy cream
Salt and freshly ground pepper
½ pound fresh mushrooms, sliced
2 tablespoons parsley, chopped

Place slices of veal between pieces of waxed paper and pound until they are ¼-inch thick.

Melt 3 tablespoons butter and 3 tablespoons oil in skillet. Sauté scallops in butter and oil for 8 to 10 minutes or until lightly browned. Transfer scallops to warm dish.

Add shallots to skillet, and sauté until tender, but not browned. Add wine and broth; stir. Bring to boil and simmer until liquid is reduced in half. Add cream, stirring. Season with salt and pepper to taste.

Sauté mushrooms in remaining butter and oil. Add mushrooms and veal to sauce. Reheat, but do not overcook. Sprinkle with parsley and serve immediately.

Serves: 6

Ragoût de Veau

3 or 4 strips bacon

2 pounds veal (shoulder, breast, or neck), cut into cubes

2 or 3 shallots, chopped

1 large green pepper, chopped

¼ cup brandy

1 tablespoon flour

½ cup white wine

1½ cups beef stock

1 cup canned Italian plum tomatoes, drained (reserve liquid)

1 clove garlic, crushed

Freshly ground pepper

Bouquet garni (4 sprigs flat parsley, 1 bay leaf, pinch of thyme)

2 stalks celery

1 pound small mushrooms, whole

Bunch of parsley, chopped

In Dutch oven, cook bacon until crisp. Remove and reserve bacon. Brown meat in bacon fat and remove with slotted spoon when browned. Add shallots and green pepper and cook for a few minutes. Add brandy and ignite to flambé. Return veal to pan and add flour. Mix well. Add wine, stock, tomatoes, garlic, and pepper. Bring to boil, reduce heat, and simmer. Add bouquet garni and celery. Cook for 1 hour and add mushrooms. Continue cooking for another 30 minutes.

If more liquid is needed, add either more stock and wine in proportion, or add reserved tomato liquid. Skim off any fat, correct seasonings, remove bouquet garni and celery, and serve with freshly chopped parsley.

Serves: 6
Special Equipment: Dutch oven

Serve this with noodles.

Roast Veal

1 4-pound boneless leg of veal
Salt and freshly ground pepper
Fresh or dry rosemary
2 bay leaves
½ teaspoon thyme
2 small onions, quartered

1 stick butter, melted
1 cup dry white wine
2 carrots, chopped
3 cloves garlic, skinned and mashed
1 tablespoon arrowroot

Preheat oven to 300 degrees.

Have veal roast larded with fat (tied on). Rub roast with salt and pepper and sprinkle with rosemary.

Place veal in roasting pan. Place meat thermometer into thickest part. Arrange onions, and carrots around roast. Season vegetables with garlic, thyme, rosemary, and bay leaves. Baste frequently with melted butter and wine, using all of both.

Remove from oven when meat thermometer reaches 145 degrees. Thicken pan juices with arrowroot.

Place veal and vegetables on platter and serve.

Serves: 6 to 8
Special Equipment: Meat thermometer

Veal Chops

. . . .

3 tablespoons olive oil

6 veal chops, about 1½ inches thick

½ cup fine dry bread crumbs

4 teaspoons tarragon, minced

2 teaspoons garlic, minced

1½ teaspoons pepper, freshly ground

1 teaspoon nutmeg, freshly grated

Rub 2 tablespoons of oil over chops.

Combine bread crumbs, tarragon, garlic, pepper and nutmeg.

Coat both sides of chops with mixture. Place in refrigerator wrapped in wax paper for 8 to 24 hours before cooking.

Drizzle remaining tablespoon of oil on chops and grill or broil chops about 5 minutes on each side for pink chops.

Serves: 6
Special Equipment: Grill

. . . .

Veal Spidini (Veal on a Spit)

1 cup fresh parsley, chopped

2 large garlic cloves, finely chopped

2 cups plain bread crumbs

½ cup Parmesan or Romano cheese, freshly grated

Olive oil, as necessary

12 slices thin veal cutlet (from leg, approximately 1½ to 2 pounds)

12 thin slices mozzarella cheese

3 slices bacon, each cut in 4 equal parts

Combine chopped parsley and garlic in bowl. Add bread crumbs and cheese and blend all together. Moisten bread crumb mixture with 4 or more tablespoons olive oil; just enough so mixture holds together without being wet.

Lay each veal slice lengthwise. Spoon on 2 tablespoons bread crumb mixture, top with 1 mozzarella slice and 1 piece bacon. Fold each long edge of veal over stuffing. Roll veal from one end to the other overlapping the two ends so that stuffing is sealed on all sides.

Put 6 veal spidinis on each skewer. Rub spidinis with olive oil and dust with leftover crumb mixture.

Broil in middle of oven on rack for 6 to 10 minutes on each side or until golden brown. Do not overcook or allow crumbs to blacken.

Serves: 6

Special Equipment: 2 long metal skewers

Veal Stew and Tagliatelle

1½ pounds stew veal from leg, cut into cubes

2 tablespoons flour

½ cup butter

3 medium onions, peeled and cut into quarters

6 tablespoons dry white wine

1 package dried Italian mushrooms (soak in water to cover, reserve liquid)

½ cup chicken stock

2 tablespoons Italian parsley, chopped

6 tablespoons heavy cream

Salt and pepper to taste

14 ounces tagliatelle or rigatoni pasta

Coat veal cubes in flour. Melt butter in large Dutch oven. Add veal and onions. Brown veal on all sides, then add white wine. Cook for approximately 2 minutes or until wine begins to evaporate. Add mushrooms plus their liquid, salt, pepper, chicken stock, and parsley.

Cover and simmer on very low heat for about 1½ hours, or until veal is almost falling apart.

Cook and drain pasta. Add heavy cream to stew mixture, stir and pour over pasta. Serve immediately.

Serves: 8
Special Equipment: Dutch oven

Fresh pasta makes this a very special dish.

Veal Zingara

1 pound veal scallops, pounded thin

Flour

1 egg, beaten

Crackermeal or plain bread crumbs

5 tablespoons olive oil

1 clove garlic, finely chopped

3 slices prosciutto, julienned

6 large fresh mushroom caps, sliced

8-ounce can artichoke hearts, drained and quartered

½ cup white wine

½ cup beef stock

Dust each piece of meat with flour, pat off excess. Dip pieces in beaten egg, then cracker meal. Set aside or refrigerate.

To prepare sauce, heat 2 tablespoons oil in large frying pan and sauté garlic until lightly browned. Remove garlic and sauté prosciutto, mushrooms, and artichokes for 2 to 3 minutes. Add wine, stock and sautéed garlic. Simmer while veal is prepared.

In another skillet, heat 3 tablespoons oil and sauté veal scallops until brown on each side, about 5 minutes.

Place veal on serving dish and pour on sauce. Serve immediately.

Serves: 4

Rack of Lamb

1 rack of lamb, about 2 pounds,
   (ask butcher to French-cut)
Salt and pepper to taste
2 teaspoons rosemary leaves,
   crushed

1½ teaspoons olive oil
1½ teaspoons parsley, chopped
2 teaspoons butter

Preheat broiler to high.

Salt and pepper lamb, rub rosemary all over it, then sprinkle with oil.

Put lamb, fat side down, on broiler pan, about 4 inches from heat. Cook about 7 minutes.

Turn lamb over. Cook for 7 minutes more.

Turn oven off and leave door open. Leave lamb in for another 7 minutes. Then take out of oven, and let rest for 5 minutes. (This results in rare to medium rare lamb).

Before serving, rub lamb with butter and parsley.

Serves: 2

Grilled Lamb Shish Kebobs

. . . .

1 7-pound leg of lamb, fat and
   gristle removed, boned, cut
   into 1-inch cubes

3 cups red onion, chopped

2 cups red wine

1 cup olive oil

1½ tablespoons salt

1 tablespoon curry powder

2 teaspoons dry mustard

1 teaspoon red pepper flakes

1 small bunch fresh mint,
   chopped

1 large green pepper, seeds
   removed, chopped

4 cloves garlic, chopped

Salt to taste

Freshly ground pepper to taste

In large bowl, combine all ingredients except lamb. Marinate meat in this mixture, covered in refrigerator for at least 12 hours, stirring occasionally.

When ready to cook, remove meat from marinade, wipe off excess, and arrange on skewers (4 or 5 pieces on each). Reserve leftover marinade.

Grill over coals or under broiler for 6 minutes, basting with marinade and turning skewers.

Serve immediately.

Serves: 10
Special Equipment: Metal skewers/Grill

This marinade is also excellent for whole leg of lamb.

. . . .

Butterflied Lamb on Grill

1 leg of lamb, butterflied
2 large yellow onions, thickly
   sliced
½ cup Worcestershire sauce
4 cloves garlic, crushed

¾ cup oil
¾ cup white or red wine
1 teaspoon dried rosemary
Freshly ground pepper to taste

Pierce meat on both sides with serving fork, place in small pan. Cover with sliced onions and freshly ground pepper. Combine remaining ingredients, pour over lamb. Cover and refrigerate for 24 hours, turning the meat at least 6 times.

Grill as you would steak, 18 minutes each side for well done, less for medium rare.

Serves: 8
Special Equipment: Grill

Glazed Spareribs

. . . .

1 rack pork spareribs (3 pounds)   2 teaspoons rosemary, minced
2 garlic cloves, minced   Salt and pepper

Glaze:
¼ cup coarse Dijon mustard   2½ tablespoons cider vinegar
1 tablespoon molasses   1½ teaspoons dry mustard
⅓ cup dark brown sugar

Preheat oven to 350 degrees.

Rub rosemary and garlic onto ribs. Salt and pepper.

Place meaty side down on baking sheet. Bake for one hour. Turn over halfway through. (Can be made one day ahead to this point. Cover with plastic and refrigerate.)

For Glaze, combine all ingredients. Bring to simmer, stir, and cool.

Place ribs on grill or under broiler, meaty side up. Spread with ⅓ of glaze. Five minutes later, turn and put on another ⅓. Turn again after 5 minutes, put on last ⅓ of glaze.

Transfer to plate. Cut into individual servings.

Serves: 2
Special Equipment: Grill

. . . .

Pork Chops and Red Cabbage

. . . .

2 pounds red cabbage, cored and shredded

1 teaspoon caraway seeds

½ cup applesauce

½ cup cranberry sauce

2 tablespoons vegetable oil

6 loin pork chops, about ¾-inch thick

Salt and pepper to taste

Preheat oven to 350 degrees.

Blanch cabbage for 2 minutes and drain. In bowl, toss cabbage with caraway seeds and pepper. Stir in applesauce and cranberry sauce. Spoon mixture into oven-proof dish.

In skillet, heat oil. Brown pork chops, sprinkle with salt and pepper, and arrange on cabbage.

Cover and bake 50 minutes, adding water if necessary to keep moist.

Serves: 4 to 6

Easy Picnic Ham

. . . .

1 cup orange juice

¾ cup light brown sugar

2 teaspoons powdered mustard

1 teaspoon ginger

2 ounces rum

1 teaspoon pumpkin or apple pie spice

1 8-pound picnic shoulder ham

Preheat oven to 325 degrees.

Mix first six ingredients and pour evenly over ham. Cover and bake for 2 hours.

Serves: 16

Chicken and Artichokes

· ·

1 3-pound chicken, cut up, or
  equivalent weight of pieces
1½ teaspoons salt
½ teaspoon pepper
½ teaspoon paprika
4 tablespoons butter
12 to 15-ounce can artichoke
  hearts

2 tablespoons butter
½ pound mushrooms, cut into
  large pieces
2 tablespoons flour
⅔ cup chicken broth
⅓ cup sherry

Preheat oven to 375 degrees.

Sprinkle chicken pieces with salt, pepper, and paprika. Brown seasoned chicken in 4 tablespoons butter. Place browned chicken into casserole dish. Cut up artichoke hearts, add to chicken.

Add 2 tablespoons butter to pan and sauté mushrooms for 5 minutes. Sprinkle flour over mushrooms and stir in chicken broth and sherry. Stir sauce over low heat until thickened.

Pour sauce over chicken, cover, and bake for 45 minutes.

Serves: 4

· ·

Chicken Cutlets in Summer Cream Sauce

6 to 8 chicken cutlets
Salt and pepper
Thyme to taste
Sage to taste
Garlic powder to taste
1 cup sour cream

1 can cream of mushroom soup
1 28-ounce can Italian plum tomatoes, drained and ¼ cup liquid reserved
6 to 8 fresh basil leaves
6 ounces mushrooms, chopped

Place cutlets in large baking dish, sprinkle liberally with salt, pepper, thyme, sage and garlic powder.

In pot combine sour cream, cream of mushroom soup, cut up plum tomatoes, reserved tomato juice, basil, and chopped mushrooms. Heat thoroughly.

Pour sauce over chicken cutlets. Cover pan with foil.

Bake at 350 degrees for 1 hour or until done.

Let sit after cooking for a few minutes to "firm."

Serves: 6

Rice, salad, asparagus, and broccoli are all good accompaniments.

Chicken Curaçao

4 chicken breasts, boned
8 chicken thighs, boned
2 tablespoons flour
Salt
1 tablespoon butter
1 tablespoon oil
¾ cup champagne

4 teaspoons Curaçao
1 cup chicken broth
1 cup fresh mushrooms
2 teaspoons melted butter
½ cup heavy cream
Mandarin orange segments
Green grapes

Preheat oven to 350 degrees.

Dredge chicken in flour and salt. Melt butter and oil in skillet, brown chicken. Place chicken in baking dish, bake for 20 minutes.

Take baking dish from oven, remove chicken with slotted spoon and set aside.

Add champagne, Curaçao, and chicken broth to skillet. Bring to slow simmer.

Return chicken to skillet, and cook over low heat for 20 minutes.

Sauté mushrooms in melted butter. Add mushrooms and cream to chicken and stir. Heat briefly.

Spoon into serving dish and garnish with orange segments and grapes.

Serves: 10

Chicken Mirepoix

3 to 4 pound chicken
1 lemon, halved
Salt and pepper to taste
1 celery stalk with leaves
½ teaspoon dried parsley
1 bayleaf
¼ teaspoon ground ginger
½ teaspoon thyme

2 green onions, green part diced
1 clove garlic
¾ pound butter, melted
1 onion, diced
1 large carrot, diced
1 stalk celery, diced
1 cup chicken stock

Preheat oven to 475 degrees. Rub chicken with salt and lemon.

Stuff cavity with celery, parsley, bayleaf, ginger, thyme, onion, and garlic. Brush with melted butter.

Place chicken in pan upside down and roast in oven for 20 minutes, remove from oven and turn breast side up. Roast for 15 minutes, basting with juices and remaining butter.

Reduce oven to 400 degrees. Remove chicken from pan and place diced onion, carrot, and celery in pan. Place chicken on top and season with salt and pepper. Pour on chicken stock. Roast 1 hour.

Remove chicken to platter. Scrape pan and pour off grease.

Place scrapings of carrot, celery, and onion in a blender. Blend until mixture reaches gravy consistency. Serve with chicken.

Serves: 8
Special Equipment: Blender

This is as appealing to the eye as to the palate.

Chicken with Raspberries and Oranges

6 chicken cutlets
Flour
Salt and pepper to taste
3 tablespoons butter
2 tablespoons vegetable oil
1 cup orange juice
½ cup dry white wine

2 tablespoons parsley
⅓ cup fresh mushrooms, sliced
4 tablespoons raspberry vinegar
⅓ cup fresh raspberries
2 oranges, sectioned and seeded
2 avocados, sliced

Dredge chicken cutlets in flour seasoned with salt and pepper.

Heat butter and oil in a skillet over medium heat. Add chicken and sauté until lightly browned on both sides. Add orange juice, wine, parsley, and mushrooms. Simmer uncovered for 5 minutes.

Transfer chicken to warm platter. Add vinegar to sauce and continue to simmer until sauce is slightly thickened (scrape up any browned bits). Add raspberries and pour over chicken.

Garnish with oranges and avocados.

Serves: 6

Honey Baked Chicken

½ cup butter

¼ cup honey

¼ cup mustard

1 teaspoon curry powder

1 teaspoon salt

2½ pounds chicken pieces

In saucepan melt butter over medium heat. Remove from heat and add honey, mix well. Add mustard, mix well. Add curry powder and salt. Pour mixture over chicken in casserole dish. Bake at 325 degrees for 1¼ hours. Baste frequently.

Serves: 6

Gravy made from drippings is quite unusual and delicious.

Indian Roast Chicken

8 to 10 chicken breasts

8 tablespoons coriander seed

1½ teaspoons ground ginger or 1 teaspoon fresh grated ginger

5 onions

1 cup yogurt

1 cup heavy cream

½ cup butter, melted

Seeds from 4 or 5 cardamom pods, crushed

1 tablespoon ground turmeric

1 teaspoon salt

Fresh ground black pepper

Preheat oven to 350 degrees. Skin breasts. Crush coriander, mix with ginger and pepper. Rub into chicken. Grate 4 onions and mix with yogurt, cream, and butter. Add cardamom seeds, turmeric, salt, and pepper. Top chicken with mixture and bake for 50 to 60 minutes, basting frequently.

Thinly slice remaining onion and place on chicken for last 10 minutes.

Serves: 6 to 8

Iri-Dori-Dumbori
(Japanese Chicken and Rice)

. . . .

1 pound chicken breast, skinned
  and boned

2 tablespoons sake

½ teaspoon salt

1 tablespoon sesame seeds

½ pound fresh snow peas (frozen
  can be used)

1 tablespoon cornstarch

2 tablespoons vegetable oil

½ cup water

4 tablespoons soy sauce

2 tablespoons mirin (sweet rice
  wine)

1 teaspoon sugar

4 cups hot cooked rice

Small jar pickled pearl onions
  (cocktail onions)

Slice chicken into approximately 1 × ½-inch pieces. Place in a bowl with sake and salt, marinate 5 to 10 minutes. Place sesame seeds in a heavy skillet over medium-high heat. Toast about 20 to 30 seconds, then mince and set aside.

String snow peas. Blanch in rapidly boiling water for 45 to 60 seconds. Drain immediately. Refresh in cold water and dry. Remove chicken from marinade and dry. In a fresh bowl, sprinkle chicken with cornstarch, tossing to coat evenly.

Heat oil in a skillet. Add chicken and sauté until pieces are white. Add water and scrape up any crusty bits sticking to bottom of pan. Reduce heat to low. Add soy sauce, mirin, and sugar. Simmer until reduced by ⅔. Increase heat for a few seconds to glaze the chicken. Sprinkle in ½ sesame seeds and mix.

To serve, put some rice in each bowl, arranging chicken on top. Arrange snow peas and several pickled onions on each serving. Sprinkle with remaining sesame seeds.

Serves: 4

. . . .

Perfect Long Island Duckling

2 Long Island ducks, close in weight

Salt and pepper to taste

1 large onion, quartered

2 stalks celery, quartered

3 cups duck sauce (available in Chinese food section) or apricot preserves

Rinse ducks well. Sprinkle insides with salt and pepper. Place onion and celery inside cavities.

Insert meat thermometer into thigh of each duck. Place ducks on rack in disposable deep oval roasting pan.

Open all vents on grill. Place 50 charcoal pieces in bottom of grill; pile them into a dome shape.

Light coals, when they are glowing, place coals in a circle around the perimeter of the grill.

Insert grill rack into correct position. Place roasting pan with ducks on top of rack. Put dome cover over all.

Every hour add 4 charcoal coals to the fire and check meat temperature. When it reaches 185 degrees, cover duck with duck sauce or apricot preserves. Ducks are done when thermometer reaches 190 degrees.

Serves: 4

Special Equipment: Grill with dome cover/2 meat thermometers

This cookbook would not be complete without a recipe for Long Island duck!

Holiday Roast Goose

1 fresh goose
1 teaspoon salt
1 teaspoon pepper

1 teaspoon sage
2 large onions, coarsely chopped
Butter

Sauce:

4 tablespoons goose fat
4 tablespoons flour
2 cups chicken broth

1 cup currant jelly
½ cup dry sherry
Salt and pepper to taste

Preheat oven to 325 degrees. Pull off and throw away excess fat from goose. Rinse out and pat dry. Place salt, pepper, sage, and onions inside cavity. Rub skin with butter, place on rack in an open pan. Do not cover.

Turn goose's position in oven once or twice to brown evenly. Remove excess fat as goose cooks and reserve. Cook about 30 minutes per pound or when meat thermometer registers 190 degrees. Goose is done when juices run clear from the leg. Let stand 30 minutes.

For sauce, put 4 tablespoons goose fat into saucepan, pour off remaining fat and discard. Save all the dark meat juices and bits in the bottom of the roasting pan.

Pour flour in saucepan, stir over medium heat until sauce turns a rich brown. Pour in chicken broth. Stir until all thickens. Pour saucepan contents into roasting pan with meat juices. Stir in scraps and brown bits from bottom of pan until dissolved. Transfer sauce back into saucepan. Heat and add currant jelly, sherry, salt, and pepper to taste.

Special Equipment: Meat thermometer

A plum pudding for dessert makes this a <u>Christmas Carol</u> feast!

Bluefish MacDonald

3 pounds whole bluefish, cleaned
Juice of 2 lemons
2 tablespoons butter
Parsley, chopped
Pepper, freshly ground

Salt
1 large yellow onion, sliced
2 large tomatoes, sliced
2 medium zucchini, sliced

Pierce fish with fork on both sides. Place in shallow, tight-fitting pan. Cover with juice of one lemon, refrigerate and marinate 2 to 3 hours.

Remove fish from pan, discard juice. Place fish on sheet of foil and cover with juice of second lemon, butter, parsley, and salt and pepper to taste. Add vegetables and wrap in foil. Grill until done, about 25 minutes.

Serves: 6
Special Equipment: Grill

Flounder Florentine

1 egg, slightly beaten
10-ounce package chopped
   spinach, cooked and well-
   drained
1½ pounds flounder filet
2 tablespoons onion, minced

1 clove garlic, minced
½ teaspoon salt
2 large tomatoes, sliced
½ cup Parmesan cheese, grated
2 tablespoons butter

Mix egg with spinach. Grease 9×13-inch pan.

Layer fish, spinach mix, onion, garlic, and salt, ending with slices of tomato. Top each tomato slice with 1 teaspoon Parmesan cheese and a dot of butter.

Bake at 350 degrees for 20 minutes until tomatoes and cheese are hot and bubbly, and fish flakes easily.

Serves: 4

Use fresh Parmesan if possible.

Charcoal Grilled Salmon Steaks

8 salmon steaks, ¾-inch thick
¾ cup dry vermouth
¾ cup olive oil
1½ tablespoons lemon juice
¾ teaspoon salt

Dash of freshly ground pepper
¼ teaspoon thyme
¼ teaspoon margarine
⅛ teaspoon sage
1 tablespoon parsley, minced

Place salmon steaks in large pan. Mix remaining ingredients and pour over steaks. Marinate for 3 to 4 hours. Turn once. Remove steaks from marinade. Reserve marinade for basting during grilling.

Place on rack close to coals on charcoal grill. Broil until brown. Turn carefully and brown other side. Cook until tender, about 15 minutes, brushing frequently with reserved marinade.

Serves: 8
Special Equipment: Grill

Salmon Steaks au Poivre with Lime Butter

....

4 1¼-inch salmon steaks
¼ cup vegetable oil
Salt to taste

1 teaspoon freeze-dried green peppercorns, crushed
4 lime wedges

Lime butter:
½ stick butter
¾ teaspoon lime rind, grated

½ teaspoon fresh lime juice

Make lime butter first. In bowl, combine butter, lime rind, and lime juice. Place mixture on sheet of waxed paper. Top with another sheet of waxed paper.

Pat mixture ¼-inch thick and chill 30 minutes or until firm. Cut into decorative shapes with small fluted cutter. Keep covered and chilled.

Rub salmon steaks on both sides with oil, salt, and peppercorns.

Heat non-stick skillet over moderate heat until hot. Sear salmon steaks 1 minute on each side. Reduce heat to moderately low and cook until salmon flakes (about 8 minutes).

Transfer to heated platter. Top with lime butter and lime wedges.

Serves: 4

Grilled Stuffed Swordfish

1 large swordfish steak (1½-inches thick)

3 tablespoons butter

1 small leek, minced

2 shallots or green onions, minced

¼ cup yellow onions, minced

4 ounces mozzarella cheese, cut in ½-inch cubes

Salt and pepper to taste

Olive oil

Using sharp knife, cut pocket into long side of swordfish steak. Do not cut completely through. Put aside.

Melt butter in skillet and sauté leeks, shallots, and onions for 5 minutes, or until soft. Put aside to cool slightly.

Add mozzarella, salt, and pepper to onions. Loosely stuff pocket with mixture. Tie kitchen string three times around fish to hold stuffing.

Brush with olive oil. Grill 3 to 6 minutes on each side, or until fish flakes easily with a fork. Remove strings before serving.

Serves: 6
Special Equipment: Grill

Broiled Lemon Scallops

2 pounds bay scallops
Salt and freshly ground pepper to
   taste
1 teaspoon dried basil

½ teaspoon dried rosemary
1 lemon, thinly sliced
Tabasco to taste
¼ cup salad oil

Wash scallops and drain. Put them in a bowl with remaining ingredients and cover. Refrigerate for 2 hours or more.

Remove scallops from marinade and arrange them in one layer in pan for broiling.

Broil approximately 3 minutes. Turn scallops over and broil for 3 minutes more or until barely cooked through. (It is important not to overcook or the scallops will toughen.)

Serve immediately.

Serves: 6

This is wonderful served over your favorite pasta.

Scallops Provencale

1 cup sweet butter, room temperature

1 cup fresh bread crumbs

6 cloves garlic, crushed

2 tablespoons onion, finely minced

½ cup fresh parsley

¼ cup white wine

Juice of ½ lemon

1 teaspoon salt

½ teaspoon pepper

2 tablespoons vegetable oil

3 tablespoons onion, minced

1½ pounds bay scallops

½ pound mushrooms, sliced

In food processor mix butter, bread crumbs, garlic, onion, parsley, wine, lemon juice, salt, and pepper. Form into ball and cover with plastic wrap. Chill garlic butter until firm, at least 1 hour.

Preheat oven to 450 degrees, grease shallow baking pan.

Sauté onion in oil until soft (not browned). Add scallops, mushrooms, salt and pepper to taste and sauté briefly.

Drain off liquid and place scallop mixture in prepared baking pan. Slice garlic butter and arrange evenly over scallops.

Bake until butter is hot and bubbly, about 5 to 10 minutes. Serve immediately.

Serves: 4
Special Equipment: Food Processor

Scallops with Tomatoes and Mushrooms

1½ pounds bay scallops

Flour

¼ cup good olive oil

4 tablespoons unsalted butter

Salt and freshly ground pepper to taste

4 tablespoons minced shallots

¼ pound fresh mushrooms

½ teaspoon thyme

2 tablespoons fresh basil, minced; or 1 large teaspoon dried

½ cup dry white wine

1 cup tomatoes, chopped

2 cloves garlic, minced

Lemon juice

Parsley

Dust scallops with flour, put single layer in large skillet. Add 3 tablespoons of oil and 1 tablespoon of butter. Season with salt and pepper. Sauté over medium heat for 3 minutes or until scallops are just firm to the touch.

Transfer the mixture to bowl and set aside.

Add remaining tablespoon of oil and 3 tablespoons of butter to skillet and melt. Add shallots, stir for one minute. Add mushrooms, thyme, basil, and salt and pepper to taste. Stir and cook for 3 minutes. Add wine and reduce over high heat to one half. Stir in tomatoes and all liquid from scallop bowl. When mixture thickens, add scallops and garlic, check seasonings.

When scallops are heated through, add lemon juice and parsley.

Serves: 4

Try serving this in a pastry shell!

Fried Softshell Crabs

. . . .

8 soft shell crabs
1 cup flour
2 eggs, beaten

2 teaspoons water
Fresh bread crumbs from 8 slices
of day-old bread

Clean and wash crabs well. Dry thoroughly. Dip them first in flour, then into beaten eggs to which water has been added. Dip in dry bread crumbs.

Fry crabs in deep, hot fat (375 degrees) until golden brown. Be careful not to overcook. Serve with hot sauce or tartar sauce and lemon wedges.

Serves: 4

. . . .

Southern Crab Cakes

2 tablespoons butter

⅔ cup green pepper, minced

⅔ cup onion, minced

⅔ cup celery, minced

2 pounds fresh crabmeat (or sea legs), shredded

¾ cup bread crumbs

⅔ cup mayonnaise

1 egg white

¼ teaspoon freshly ground pepper

Dash hot pepper sauce

Fine bread crumbs

½ cup butter

Melt 2 tablespoons butter in skillet, add green pepper, onion, and celery. Cover and cook until soft, about 10 minutes. Cool slightly.

Line 2 baking sheets with wax paper.

Mix vegetables with crabmeat, bread crumbs, mayonnaise, and egg white in large bowl. Add pepper and hot sauce.

Shape generous tablespoonsful into 2-inch patties, 1-inch thick. Coat with bread crumbs. Arrange on baking sheets, chill overnight.

Preheat oven to 425 degrees. Brush 2 baking sheets with 1 tablespoon butter. Arrange crab cakes on baking sheets. Drizzle lightly with remaining butter.

Bake until cakes are heated (5 to 7 minutes) through and tops are brown and crisp. Broil cakes 1 minute if tops are not browned. Drain on paper towels and serve.

Yield: 24 Crab Cakes

This could also be used as a delicious fish stuffing.

Chinese Ginger Shrimp

2 stalks celery, cut into ½-inch slices

8-ounce can bamboo shoots, drained

¼ cup scallions, chopped

¼ cup white wine vinegar

2 tablespoons soy sauce

5 teaspoons sugar

1 teaspoon cornstarch

3 tablespoons salad oil

2 cloves garlic, minced

2 teaspoons fresh ginger, grated

1 pound medium-sized shrimp, peeled and deveined

1 scallion, thinly sliced

In bowl, combine celery, bamboo, and scallions. Set aside.

In another bowl, stir together vinegar, soy sauce, sugar, and cornstarch. Set aside.

Heat 2 tablespoons oil in large skillet over medium heat. Add garlic and ginger and stir once.

Add shrimp and stir-fry until pink on outside (4 to 5 minutes). Remove from pan. Set aside.

Add rest of oil to pan. Add vegetables and stir-fry for 1 minute. Return shrimp to pan.

Stir vinegar mix once; add to pan. Cook, stirring until sauce bubbles and thickens (about 1 minute).

Garnish with sliced scallion.

Serves: 4

Shrimp Sautéed in Herb Butter

1 pound raw shrimp, peeled and deveined

1 tablespoon parsley, chopped

1 to 2 garlic cloves, minced

½ teaspoon tarragon leaves

½ teaspoon dry mustard

¾ teaspoon salt

⅛ teaspoon red pepper, crushed

¼ cup butter

1 tablespoon cooking oil

2 tablespoons lemon juice

1 tablespoon Worcestershire sauce

3 cups cooked rice

Pinch of saffron

Combine all seasonings, except saffron, in a small bowl.

Ten minutes before serving, melt butter with oil in heavy skillet. Add lemon juice and seasonings. Sauté shrimp in skillet over medium heat for 8 minutes, or until shrimp is pink. Turn once.

Serve over rice to which a pinch of powdered saffron has been added.

Serves: 6

Shrimp Jambalaya

3 pounds large shrimp, peeled
and deveined

¾ cup butter or oil

Garlic powder to taste

1 cup onion, minced

1½ cups canned Italian plum
tomatoes, chopped

3 green peppers, diced

1½ red bell peppers, diced

3 cups raw rice

6 to 8 cups chicken broth

Cayenne pepper to taste, about 2
dashes

3 bay leaves

¾ teaspoon thyme

¾ cup flat parsley, chopped

1 tablespoon salt

Fresh ground pepper

1 teaspoon saffron

1 small package peas, frozen

Pimento strips as garnish

Pitted black olives as garnish

In a large skillet, sauté shrimp in butter or oil for approximately 2 to 3 minutes, until pink. Sprinkle garlic powder in butter, to taste. Remove shrimp, set aside, and keep warm.

In pan drippings, sauté onions, plum tomatoes, green pepper, and red pepper. Add raw rice, stir.

Cover rice with chicken broth, add cayenne, bay leaves, thyme, parsley, salt, pepper, saffron, and peas.

Simmer about 20 minutes until rice is done and liquid is absorbed. Stir occasionally.

Place shrimp on rice and serve.

Garnish with pimento and olives if desired.

Serves: 8 to 10

Shrimp Scampi

½ cup olive oil

3 tablespoons garlic, finely chopped

1 pound large shrimp, peeled and deveined, with tails

3 tablespoons butter

¼ cup freshly squeezed lemon juice

¼ cup parsley, finely chopped

In a large skillet, heat oil. Sauté garlic until light brown; do not burn. Add shrimp, butter, and lemon juice. Cook until shrimp are firm and pink (about 2 or 3 minutes). Add parsley, toss slightly, and serve.

Serves: 2 to 4

Serve over a bed of linguine.

Spicy Shrimp

1 pound shrimp, peeled and
   deveined

1 tablespoon cornstarch

1 egg white

2 cups water mixed with 2
   tablespoons vegetable oil

1 tablespoon vegetable oil

1 tablespoon ginger, minced

1 tablespoon garlic, minced

1 teaspoon sesame oil

Sauce mixture:

1 tablespoon sugar

1 teaspoon salt

1 tablespoon rice wine or sherry

1 tablespoon hot bean paste*

3 tablespoons ketchup

Pat shrimp dry. Marinate at least 30 minutes in cornstarch and egg white mixture or marinate in the refrigerator a day ahead.

Prepare sauce by combining indicated ingredients in a bowl.

Bring water and oil to a boil. Add shrimp and cook until just pink. Drain.

Heat 1 tablespoon vegetable oil in wok or heavy frying pan. Add ginger and garlic, stir until fragrant. Add sauce, mix well. Add shrimp, mix well. Turn off heat.

Dribble on sesame oil. Mix well and serve immediately.

Serves: 3 to 4; 6 as side dish
Special Equipment: Wok (optional)

Excellent as part of a buffet.

* available in gourmet or oriental section of supermarket

Clams Posillipo

2 tablespoons olive oil

4 garlic cloves, minced

2 small bottles clam juice

2 28-ounce cans crushed plum tomatoes with tomato paste

1 cup dry white wine

½ cup sweet butter

½ teaspoon salt

2 teaspoons oregano, dried

2 teaspoons basil, dried

2 teaspoons rosemary, dried

¼ cup parsley, finely chopped

6 dozen little neck clams, well scrubbed

2 pounds pasta

In a large stock pot, heat olive oil over medium heat until haze forms. Add garlic and sauté until golden. Remove from heat and add remaining ingredients except clams.

Return to heat and simmer for approximately 2 hours. Add clams and cover for 5 to 10 minutes or until all clams are open. When clams are open, remove from heat. Let stand 5 minutes.

Serve in soup dishes over linguine or spaghetti.

Serves: 6 to 8

Microwave Coquilles Saint Jacques

1 pound bay scallops
3 tablespoons butter
4 scallions or 1 small onion, chopped
1 clove garlic, minced
1 tablespoon parsley, chopped
¼ teaspoon thyme
12 fresh mushrooms, sliced
½ cup dry vermouth or white wine

Salt and pepper, to taste
2 tablespoons flour
2 tablespoons butter
¼ cup water
2 tablespoons lemon juice
¼ cup heavy cream
½ cup dried bread crumbs
Paprika

In 2 quart casserole, melt 3 tablespoons butter with onion, garlic, parsley and thyme. Microwave on high for 2 minutes until onion is tender. Stir in scallops, mushrooms, wine. Microwave on high for 2 minutes.

While mixture is cooking, blend 2 tablespoons butter with flour in measuring cup; stir in water and lemon juice to make paste. Blend in cream. Add this to scallops and mushrooms and stir. Microwave 2 minutes until sauce thickens. Scallops should be firm but not hard. Add salt and pepper.

Spoon mixture into scalloped serving shells or ramekins. Sprinkle with bread crumbs and paprika. Place 3 or 4 shells at a time in microwave, heat on high for 2 to 3 minutes until hot.

Remove and cover with foil to keep warm while heating additional shells, or place all on cookie sheet under broiler of conventional oven to brown lightly. Serve with lemon slices, sprig of parsley.

Serves: 4
Special Equipment: Microwave oven

Paella a la Valenciana

3 pounds chicken breasts and thighs

1 pound lean pork, cubed

½ pound chorizos, or other smoked sausage, cut into ½-inch slices

½ cup olive oil

1 teaspoon paprika

3 whole garlic cloves

2 medium onions, minced

2 tablespoons parsley, minced

1 pimento, drained and chopped

1 teaspoon saffron

1 teaspoon salt

1 tablespoon warm water

2 cups rice

3½ cups chicken broth

2 pounds shrimp, shelled and deveined

2 dozen mussels, scrubbed well

2 dozen Little Neck clams, cleaned

1 cup frozen tiny peas

Sauté chicken, pork, and smoked sausage in olive oil until crispy and brown. Sprinkle with paprika. Add garlic cloves and a handful of onions to pan as meat and chicken brown. Remove meat and chicken to either a paella pan or a large casserole, and set aside garlic in a small bowl. To the sauté pan, add parsley and remaining onion. Sauté, add pimento and more olive oil if needed.

In small bowl, crush saffron with browned garlic and salt. Stir in warm water to dissolve and add to sauté pan. Add rice to sauté pan mixture and stir to glaze. Slowly add chicken broth and bring to boil. Pour rice mixture over browned meat in paella pan or large casserole dish. Add shrimp, mussels, clams, and peas. Stir to distribute.

Bake uncovered at 350 degrees until liquid is absorbed, but mixture is not dry, about 25 minutes.

Serves: 8 to 12
Special Equipment: Paella pan

Sea Cliff Train Station

Eggs, Cheese & Pasta

"Tennis Whites Preferred"

"Cradle of Aviation", site of some of the country's earliest turnpikes, home to the nation's largest commuter railroad . . . Long Islanders have always been on the move. The early settlers had to rely on ferries to leave the Island. Today, twelve bridges and tunnels connect us to our neighbors, while ferries still transport us to Connecticut, Rhode Island, and our own South Shore barrier islands. The general pattern of Long Island roads was established in 1773 and the succeeding years saw hundreds of turnpikes, parkways, and expressways fit into the plan. Motorists caught in our infamous traffic snarls often wish early highway designers had better anticipated the needs of eight million mobile residents.

Trains were an early attempt to provide mass transportation. At one time there were 30 different railroads on Long Island. By 1882, these had been combined into the Long Island Railroad, a system that now carries an average of 280,000 passengers per day, making it the nation's largest commuter railroad.

By 1900, booming prosperity made it tough to keep our feet on the ground. The American aviation industry was born on the same Hempstead plains that were home to the early settlers. The first U.S. Airmail flight originated there in 1911 and Charles Lindbergh began his historic transatlantic flight from Roosevelt Field in 1927. Curtiss Aviation in Garden City built the most U.S. fighter planes during World War I and Republic Aviation in Farmingdale matched this mark during World War II. Today, Grumman Aviation is a leading military aerospace producer and was the manufacturer of the Lunar Excursion Module from which Neil Armstrong made his historic "one small step".

Seafood Pasta

2 cups fresh mushrooms, sliced
  (6 ounces)

4 shallots, finely chopped

½ cup butter

1½ cups Madeira wine

1 tablespoon tomato paste

1 tablespoon tarragon, freshly
  snipped or 1 teaspoon dried,
  crushed

¼ teaspoon salt

Dash pepper, freshly ground

10 ounces linguine

1½ pounds fresh shrimp, shelled
  and deveined

4 cups water

1½ cups heavy cream

2 egg yolks

Salt and pepper, freshly ground

In a skillet, sauté mushrooms and shallots in butter over medium heat for 4 to 5 minutes until tender, but not brown. Remove with slotted spoon and set aside.

Stir wine, tomato paste, tarragon, salt, and pepper into butter remaining in skillet. Bring to boil. Boil vigorously for 10 minutes or until mixture is reduced to ½ cup.

Meanwhile, cook pasta according to package directions. Drain. Keep warm. Drop fresh shrimp into boiling water, return to boil. Reduce heat and simmer for 1-3 minutes or until shrimp turn pink. Drain. Keep warm.

In a bowl, stir together heavy cream and the egg yolks. Add the wine mixture. Return to skillet, cook and stir until thickened. Stir in shrimp, mushrooms, and shallots, heat thoroughly. Season to taste with salt and pepper. Toss with cooked pasta. Transfer to serving platter.

Serves: 4 to 6

Nice for a first course or casual entree.

Chicken Scampi with Linguine

1 pound chicken breasts, boned and skinned

1 egg, beaten

1 cup seasoned bread crumbs

2 tablespoons butter

⅓ cup vegetable oil

1 pound package linguine

½ cup butter

3 cloves garlic, minced

1 tablespoon lemon juice

½ teaspoon salt

¼ teaspoon pepper

2 tablespoons butter

¼ cup chopped parsley

Lemon wedges

Cut chicken into ½-inch pieces. Dip pieces in beaten egg.

Combine bread crumbs, salt, and pepper in large plastic storage bag. Add chicken pieces a few at a time and shake in bag until well coated. Spread coated pieces on a platter. (These first three steps can be done ahead of time and the chicken refrigerated).

Heat oil and butter in large skillet. Add ⅓ of chicken and sauté until golden brown. Repeat with remaining pieces. Discard oil and wipe out skillet. Cook linguine according to package directions.

While pasta is cooking, melt ½ cup butter in skillet. Cook garlic for 1 minute; add chicken, lemon juice, salt, and pepper. Toss so chicken is coated with sauce, but do not allow chicken to cook further.

Drain linguine, toss with remaining 2 tablespoons butter, and spoon onto heated platter. Spoon chicken and sauce over pasta. Sprinkle with parsley and serve with lemon wedges.

Serves: 4

Pasta with Black Olives and Tomato Sauce

Olive oil

2 or 3 cloves garlic, finely chopped

28-ounce can Italian peeled tomatoes

16-ounce can black pitted olives, drained and sliced

8-ounce can tomato sauce

1 pound small pasta shells

1 pound mozzarella cheese, diced

5 slices bacon, cooked and crumbled

Parmesan cheese, grated

Parsley, finely chopped

Sauté garlic in a pan coated with olive oil. Add Italian peeled tomatoes (break big tomato chunks apart with wooden spoon) and simmer for 30 minutes. Stir in olives and tomato sauce. Simmer about 1 to 1½ hours or until sauce thickens.

Cook small shells according to directions on package and drain. On a serving platter or bowl, layer sauce, shells, and mozzarella cheese. Top with remaining sauce and sprinkle with bacon and Parmesan cheese. Top with parsley.

Serves: 4 to 6

A Very Special Mushroom Cannelloni

Pasta (or use fresh from store):

4 eggs, beaten

2⅔ cups flour

4 pinches salt

1 tablespoon water

Sauce:

1 stick butter

⅔ cup flour

4¼ cups milk, heated (do not boil)

¼ cup Parmesan cheese, freshly grated

1 teaspoon salt

Filling:

3 tablespoons butter

3 tablespoons olive oil

2 12-ounce containers mushrooms, cleaned, trimmed, and sliced

4 whole cloves garlic, peeled, and left whole

Other:

4 tablespoons butter (for pans)

½ cup Parmesan cheese, freshly grated

1 cup Swiss cheese, shredded

1 cup ham, ground or finely chopped in food processor

4 tablespoons butter (for topping)

Pasta: Mix all ingredients together with a fork and knead until smooth and very elastic. Wrap dough in plastic and let rest at least 1 hour. You may mix dough the night before and store in refrigerator.

Continued on next page

Roll dough into 4 6-inch wide lasagna noodle strips, following pasta machine instructions. Cut each long strip into strips 3 inches wide, dust with flour and dry slightly on floured towels. Boil in batches until barely tender and remove to large bowl of cold water. Leave pasta in cold water until ready to pat dry and fill.

Sauce: Melt butter over medium heat. Add flour and stir. Add milk and whisk until smooth. Cook until thickened (5 to 10 minutes). Add Parmesan and salt. Remove from heat. Place 3 cups of sauce in separate bowl. This will be used in final assembly. Leave the rest of the sauce in pan to cool.

Filling: Melt butter and oil in large pan. Add mushrooms and garlic and cook until mushrooms are limp and most moisture has cooked away. Discard garlic cloves. Chop mushrooms finely in food processor and add to cooled sauce which was left in sauce pan.

Spread each of 2 lasagna pans with 2 tablespoons butter and ¼ cup Parmesan. Remove 10 pasta strips from cold water and pat dry. Place 2 heaping teaspoons of filling at one end of each pasta strip and roll up. Place rolls in prepared pan. When both pans are filled, sprinkle shredded Swiss cheese evenly over both, then sprinkle ground ham over cheese.

Continued on next page

Continued *A Very Special Mushroom Cannelloni*

Pour reserved 3 cups of sauce evenly over both pans (you may add milk if it is too thick to pour). Be sure to pour sauce to edges of cannelloni or it will dry out during baking. Dot top of each casserole with small pieces of butter (2 tablespoons per pan). Freeze, refrigerate or cook immediately. If frozen, defrost 24 hours in refrigerator before baking.

Bake, covered with foil, at 325 degrees for 20 to 40 minutes. Be careful not to overcook. Pour milk over edges of pasta if is drying but center is not yet warm.

Serves: 8 to 10
Special Equipment: Pasta machine/Food Processor

Well worth the effort — can be frozen too!

Fettuccine and Crab

¼ pound butter
2 to 3 cloves garlic, crushed
1 pound crab meat
Juice of ½ lemon

1 pound fettuccine, cooked and drained
Parmesan cheese, grated
Fresh parsley

Melt butter and sauté garlic. Add crab meat and heat through. Stir in lemon juice and cook, stirring, for one minute. Pour over noodles and toss. Sprinkle with cheese and garnish with fresh parsley. Serve immediately.

Serves: 4

Pasta with Shrimp and Broccoli

3 ounces olive oil
3 cloves garlic, chopped
½ pound shrimp, peeled and deveined
2 cups broccoli, flowers and sliced stems

6 plum tomatoes, chopped
3 ounces chicken stock
Fresh basil, to taste
12 ounces bow tie pasta

Heat olive oil. Add garlic, shrimp, broccoli, and tomatoes. Sauté 2 to 3 minutes, stirring. Add chicken stock and sauté for 3 minutes. Add basil. Prepare pasta according to directions and drain. Pour sauce over pasta and serve.

Serves: 4

Angel Hair Pasta with Fresh Tomato Sauce

....

Sauce:

2 pounds very ripe tomatoes, plum, if possible

1 small onion, minced

½ cup fresh basil, chopped

½ cup olive oil

2 cloves garlic, minced

Salt and pepper, to taste

1 pound angel hair pasta (cappellini)

½ cup Parmesan cheese, grated

Drop tomatoes into boiling water. Remove after 1 minute. When cool enough to handle, peel, seed, and chop coarsely.

In a bowl, mix tomatoes with onion, basil, oil, garlic, salt, and pepper. Let sit at room temperature at least 1 hour before serving.

Cook pasta in boiling salted water until al dente. Drain. In a large bowl, toss pasta with tomato sauce and cheese — serve immediately. Serve with additional cheese.

Serves: 4 to 6

....

Gold Coast Primavera

1 bunch broccoli, florets only

2 small zucchini, cut in ¼-inch slices

½ cup carrots, diced

1 pound linguine

1 garlic clove, chopped

1 pint cherry tomatoes, halved

¼ cup olive oil

¼ cup basil, chopped or 1 teaspoon dried

½ pound mushrooms, sliced

½ cup peas

Salt and pepper

½ teaspoon crushed red pepper, optional

½ stick butter

¾ cup heavy cream

¾ cup Parmesan cheese, freshly grated

Cook broccoli, zucchini, and carrots separately until just tender. Drain. Put in large bowl.

Cook and drain linguine. Keep warm.

Sauté garlic and tomatoes in oil in a large skillet, about 3 minutes. Stir in basil and mushrooms, cook 3 minutes. Stir in peas, salt, pepper, and red pepper, cook 1 minute. Add to vegetables in bowl.

Melt butter in same skillet. Add cream and cheese, stirring constantly until smooth. Add linguine, toss to coat.

Stir in vegetables, heat for 2 to 3 minutes.

Serve immediately.

Serves: 6

Rigatoni with Ham, Tomatoes and Fresh Basil

. . . .

⅓ cup ham fat, finely chopped

4 cloves garlic, minced

1 tablespoon olive oil

2 tablespoons fresh parsley, chopped

2 pounds fresh tomatoes, cubed (can substitute canned)

Salt and pepper to taste

1 to 3 pounds ham, cubed (left over baked is the best)

14 ounces rigatoni-type pasta

15 to 20 leaves fresh basil (torn with your fingers)

¼ cup Parmesan cheese, grated

Chop ham fat, garlic, oil and parsley together in food processor to make a paste. Transfer to pan and sauté over low heat for approximately 10 minutes. Add tomatoes, salt, and pepper to mixture. Cook for 15 minutes or until soft. Add ham and cook 7 minutes longer.

Cook pasta well and drain. Pour sauce over pasta, add fresh basil, and mix throughly. Sprinkle with Parmesan cheese.

Serves: 4 to 6
Special Equipment: Food Processor

. . . .

Summer Linguine

4 large tomatoes, peeled and cut in ½-inch cubes

1 pound Brie cheese, rind removed, torn in pieces

1 cup cleaned fresh basil leaves, cut in strips

3 garlic cloves, peeled, finely minced

1 cup plus 1 tablespoon best quality olive oil

2½ teaspoons salt

½ teaspoon freshly ground black pepper

1½ pounds linguine

Parmesan cheese, freshly grated

Whole basil leaves to garnish

Combine tomatoes, Brie, basil, garlic, 1 cup olive oil, ½ teaspoon salt, and pepper in large bowl. Do this 2 hours before serving. Leave covered at room temperature.

Bring 6 quarts of water to a boil. Add 1 tablespoon olive oil and remaining salt. Cook linguine until al dente, 8 to 10 minutes. Drain pasta and toss with tomato sauce. Serve with Parmesan cheese and a few grinds of fresh pepper. Serve garnished with whole basil leaves.

Serves: 6

Pastitsio

. . . .

2 tablespoons vegetable oil

2 medium-sized onions, chopped

2 cloves garlic, minced

1 pound lean ground beef or
   lamb

8 ounces tomato sauce

2 tablespoons tomato paste

1 teaspoon salt

½ teaspoon cinnamon

1 pound ziti

2 tablespoons butter

1 cup (4 ounces) grated
   Parmesan or Romano cheese

4 egg whites, slightly beaten

Béchamel Sauce:

6 tablespoons butter

¾ cup flour

3 cups milk

10¾-ounces condensed chicken
   broth

¾ teaspoon salt

⅛ teaspoon pepper

4 egg yolks, slightly beaten

Heat oil in large skillet over medium-high heat. Sauté onion and garlic until golden. Add ground meat and brown; drain off excess fat. Stir in tomato sauce, tomato paste, salt, and cinnamon. Reduce heat, cover, and simmer 20 minutes.

Béchamel Sauce: In large saucepan, melt butter over medium heat. Add flour, stirring until completely blended and smooth. Remove from heat. Gradually stir in milk and broth. Return to heat; cook, stirring constantly until mixture thickens and comes to a boil.

Stir in salt and pepper. Remove sauce from heat; blend egg yolks into hot sauce one at a time, stirring well after each addition.

Continued on next page

. . . .

Cook ziti as package directs. Drain and toss with butter, ¾ cup grated cheese and egg whites.

Preheat oven to 350 degrees. Spoon half the ziti into bottom of shallow 3 quart casserole or lasagna pan. Spoon on meat mixture. Cover with remaining ziti.

Pour Béchamel sauce over top of casserole (clear a few "passages" so sauce can reach bottom layer). Sprinkle top with remaining cheese. Bake 45 minutes until browned and bubbly. Cool about 10 minutes and serve.

Serves: 6 to 8

Pasta Carbonara

1 pound bacon, chopped in
   1-inch pieces
1 stick sweet butter
1 medium onion, chopped
1 cup light cream
1 egg, lightly beaten

1 cup Parmesan cheese, grated
½ cup Italian parsley, chopped
1 pound spaghetti or linguine
¾ cup chicken broth, heated
Pepper, freshly ground

Cook bacon until lightly brown. (If using a microwave oven, cook 4 minutes on high, drain, then cook another 3 to 4 minutes.) Sauté onion in butter until onion is a light brown.

In small bowl, combine cream, egg, ⅔ cup Parmesan cheese, and parsley. Set aside.

Cook pasta according to instructions on package. Drain. Return pasta to pot and add onion mixture, cream mixture, bacon, broth, and freshly ground pepper. Serve immediately with remaining cheese.

Serves: 4
Special Equipment: Microwave (optional)

An excellent dinner for ski country!

Pasta with Smoked Salmon and Dill

½ cup dry white wine
3 tablespoons shallots, chopped
1½ cups heavy cream
¼ teaspoon cayenne pepper
Pinch of nutmeg
1 twist lemon rind

¼ cup butter, melted
1 pound smoked salmon, cut in
  2½-inch strips
1 pound pasta: tagliatelle,
  rigatoni or fettuccine
1 to 2 tablespoons fresh dill

Bring wine to a boil. Add shallots. Boil until liquid is reduced to 2 tablespoons. Add cream, cayenne, nutmeg, and lemon rind. Cook over low heat 5 minutes. Add melted butter and salmon pieces, heat thoroughly.

Cook pasta according to package directions and drain. Remove to warm dish. Remove lemon rind from sauce. Pour over pasta. Sprinkle with snipped fresh dill.

Serves: 4

Pasta with Broccoli and Sun Dried Tomatoes

....

1 pound pasta, penne or linguine

3 tablespoons olive oil

2 cloves garlic, chopped

1 bunch broccoli, florets only, lightly steamed

2 tablespoons pignoli nuts, toasted

4 tablespoons Parmesan cheese, grated

2 ounces sun dried tomatoes, chopped

Salt and pepper to taste

Cook pasta according to package directions. Keep warm. Heat olive oil. Sauté garlic. Add broccoli, toasted nuts, 2 tablespoons cheese, and tomatoes. Blend all with pasta. Season to taste. Sprinkle remaining cheese on top.

Serves: 4

....

Tortellini with Gorgonzola Sauce

....

1½ cups dry white wine	1½ pounds green tortellini
8 ounces cream cheese, softened	1½ tablespoons Parmesan cheese, grated
Dash ground pepper	
Large pinch nutmeg	¾ pound gorgonzola cheese

In small sauce pan, heat wine until it boils. Cook over high heat until wine reduces to ¾ cup. With a wire whisk, blend in cream cheese until smooth. Heat to a boil, then reduce heat and simmer 15 minutes uncovered. Stir in pepper and nutmeg.

Cook tortellini and drain. Blend Parmesan and one half gorgonzola cheese into the cream sauce. Pour sauce over tortellini, sprinkle rest of gorgonzola on top.

Serves: 6

Brie Soufflé

· ·

6 tablespoons sweet butter, room temperature

6 slices of good quality white bread, crusts removed

1½ cups milk

1 teaspoon salt

Dash Tabasco

3 eggs

1 pound slightly underripe Brie, rind removed

Preheat oven to 350 degrees. Butter a 1½ quart soufflé dish. Butter one side of bread slices and cut each slice into thirds. Whisk together milk, salt, Tabasco, and eggs. Coarsely grate the Brie.

Arrange half the bread, buttered side up on the bottom of the dish. Sprinkle evenly with half the Brie. Repeat with remaining bread and Brie. Carefully pour the egg mixture over the bread. Let stand at room temperature for 30 minutes. Bake 25 to 30 minutes or until bubbling and golden.

Serves: 4 to 6
Special Equipment: Soufflé Dish

· ·

Spicy Sausage Quiche

1 9" pie crust, partially baked
½ pound bulk pork sausage
½ cup fresh mushrooms, sliced
½ cup onion, chopped
4 ounce can green chili peppers,
    chopped
¼ teaspoon dried basil leaves

¼ teaspoon chili powder
1 cup cheddar cheese, shredded
3 eggs, beaten
1½ cups half and half
½ teaspoon salt
⅛ teaspoon pepper

Crumble sausage into frying pan and cook until no longer pink. Add mushrooms, onion, peppers, basil, and chili powder, mixing well. Drain. Sprinkle cheese into pie shell and top with sausage mixture.

Combine eggs, half and half, salt, and pepper and mix well. Pour egg mixture over sausage. Bake at 350 degrees for 30 to 35 minutes.

Serves: 6 to 8

Cheese Soufflé

. . . .

½ cup butter
½ cup flour
2 cups milk, heated (do not boil)
½ teaspoon salt
¼ teaspoon pepper

½ teaspoon dry mustard
8 eggs, separated
2 cups cheddar cheese, grated
Parsley

Melt butter. Add flour and stir. Let flour and butter bubble together for 2 minutes. Remove from heat. Add milk all at once. Return to medium heat and stir until thickened. Season with salt, pepper and dry mustard. Remove from heat. Add egg yolks one at a time, stirring well after each addition. Add cheese. Beat egg whites until stiff but not dry. Fold into cheese mixture.

Pour into unbuttered 2-quart soufflé or casserole dish. Bake at 350 degrees for 50 to 60 minutes or until golden brown. Do not open oven for first 30 minutes of baking time. Garnish with parsley.

Serves: 6
Special Equipment: Soufflé dish

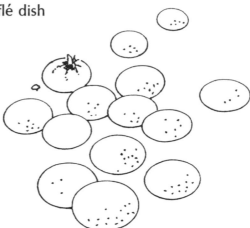

. . . .

Egg Puff Casserole

1 box seasoned croutons
1½ cups cheddar cheese, grated
1 cup Swiss cheese, grated
1 cup jalapeño pepper cheese, grated
1 pound bacon or sausage (browned, drained and crumbled) or diced ham

8 eggs
1 pint half and half
1½ cups milk
1½ teaspoons dry mustard
Salt and pepper to taste
Dash onion powder

Grease 9×13-inch pan. Cover bottom of pan with seasoned croutons. Layer cheeses and meat over croutons.

Beat eggs and add half and half and milk. To milk mixture, add mustard, salt, pepper, and onion powder. Pour over layers. Cover with plastic wrap and refrigerate overnight.

Bake at 325 degrees for 35 to 45 minutes until set and lightly browned.

Serves: 8
Special Equipment: 9×13-inch pan

Swiss Pie Florentine with Cheese Crust

. . . .

Cheese crust:

1¼ cups sharp cheddar cheese, shredded

¾ cup flour

1 teaspoon salt

¼ teaspoon dry mustard

¼ cup butter, melted

Filling:

½ cup onion, finely chopped

1½ cups fresh mushrooms, sliced

¼ cup butter

¼ cup flour

½ cup heavy cream

½ cup milk

1 10-ounce package chopped frozen spinach, cooked and well-drained

1 teaspoon salt

¼ teaspoon nutmeg

Dash of pepper

3 eggs, slightly beaten

Cheese crust: Combine cheese, flour, and seasonings. Add melted butter. Mix well. Pat into a 9-inch pie pan.

Sauté chopped onion and mushrooms in butter. Stir in flour and cook for 3 to 4 minutes. Add cream and milk and cook, stirring constantly until thickened. Add spinach to cream mixture. Add seasoning and eggs and mix well.

Pour spinach cheese mixture into cheese crust. Bake at 400 degrees for 15 minutes. Reduce heat to 325 degrees. Bake 25 minutes longer or until done.

Serves: 6

. . . .

North Shore Vineyard

Vegetables, Rice & Accompaniments

"Ground Strokes"

Farming was the first occupation of Long Island settlers. The climate, and a growing season of 200 days per year, make Suffolk County the most productive agricultural region in New York State. Garden crops, potatoes, ducks, and ornamental plants dominate the profitable Long Island agriculture business today.

Our most famous product is the Long Island Kahtadin cooking potato. Once one of the largest potato producing areas in the country, increasingly populated Suffolk County still devotes 9,000 acres to potato farming. Ducks are a close second for celebrity product status. Long Island duckling is considered a delicacy around the world for its tender, meaty flesh. In 1988, duck farmers delivered two and a half million of the pudgy quackers to gourmets' tables.

In total dollars, commercial garden crops such as strawberries, raspberries, asparagus, and cauliflower actually account for the greatest agricultural income on the Island. Ornamental nursery stock, flower beds and sod farms cover almost 10,000 acres. In recent years, wine-making has made a significant and nationally recognized comeback, earning coveted awards for several vineyards.

Long Island's productivity is not limited to animals and vegetables. We are further blessed with the minds, money, and materials to make us the fourth-largest industrial region in the U.S. Key industries are shipping, aerospace, and nuclear research, while new high-tech firms are rapidly establishing Long Island as the Silicon Valley of the East. Other important industries include apparel, specialized food processing, machinery, and electrical equipment

Elva's Calico Beans

½ pound ham, cubed and browned

½ pound bacon, cooked and drained

1 16-ounce can butter beans, drained

1 16-ounce can kidney beans, drained

1 16-ounce can pork and beans, with liquid

½ cup ketchup

¼ cup vinegar

¾ cup brown sugar

1 teaspoon dry mustard

1 teaspoon salt

½ medium onion, chopped

Combine all ingredients. Put into crockpot. Cook on low for 4 hours. You may also put ingredients into covered casserole and bake at 350 degrees for 1½ hours.

Serves: 6 to 8
Special Equipment: Crockpot (optional)

Great with burgers.

Mrs. Deasy's Carrots

1 pound carrots, scraped and cut in ¼-inch slices

2 tablespoons onion, minced

½ cup mayonnaise

1½ tablespoons prepared horseradish

2 tablespoons butter or margarine, cut into small pieces

Parsley (optional)

2 tablespoons butter or margarine, melted

½ cup breadcrumbs

Cook carrots in small amount of salted water until just tender. Drain, reserving ¼ cup of water. Put carrots in well-buttered casserole.

In small bowl, mix together onion, mayonnaise, horseradish and carrot juice. Pour over carrots. Dot with butter and sprinkle with parsley. Mix melted butter with bread crumbs and spread over vegetables. Bake at 350 degrees for 15 to 30 minutes until lightly browned and bubbly.

Serves: 4

Cauliflower with Broccoli Sauce

1 head cauliflower	Salt and pepper to taste
1 head broccoli	Lemon juice (optional)
3 tablespoons sour cream	Nutmeg (optional)
4 tablespoons butter	1 cup breadcrumbs tossed with 4
4 tablespoons grated Parmesan cheese	to 5 tablespoons melted butter
	Butter

Prepare cauliflower by separating into florets and discarding any tough stems.

Cook in 3 quarts boiling, salted water until crisp and tender, about 7 minutes. Drain and rinse under cold water (refresh) to stop cooking. Drain well.

Prepare broccoli the same way. Cook it in 3 quarts boiling, salted water, about 5 minutes. Drain and refresh.

Place warm broccoli in food processor with sour cream, 3 tablespoons butter and 2 tablespoons cheese, salt and pepper to taste. Blend until very smooth. Add lemon juice and nutmeg if desired.

Arrange drained cauliflower in well-buttered baking dish. Season with salt and pepper and sprinkle with remaining cheese as vegetable is layered in dish.

Pour broccoli purée over cauliflower; top with bread crumbs and dot with butter. Bake at 350 degrees for 20 minutes.

Serves: 4
Special Equipment: Food Processor

Dill Cucumbers Sauté

6 cucumbers, peeled and cut in
  ¼-inch slices
1 tablespoon salt
¾ cup butter

¼ cup fresh dill, chopped
Salt and pepper and additional
  butter to taste

Place prepared cucumbers in bowl and toss with salt. Let stand for 30 minutes. Drain well and pat excess liquid from cucumbers with paper towel.

In skillet with cover, melt butter. Add cucumbers, cover, and cook over low heat for 10 minutes or until cucumbers become translucent. Add dill and additional butter, salt, and pepper to taste.

Serves: 8

Baked Spinach

3 10-ounce packages frozen
  chopped spinach
3 tablespoons butter
6 shallots, finely chopped
¾ cup heavy cream

4 eggs, beaten
10 tablespoons grated Parmesan
  cheese
½ cup water chestnuts, chopped

Cook spinach according to package instructions. Drain, put in colander and squeeze dry. Melt butter and sauté shallots for 6 minutes.

Mix drained spinach with shallots, heavy cream, eggs, cheese, and water chestnuts in large bowl. Put into shallow buttered casserole. Bake at 400 degrees for 10 minutes.

Serves: 8

Fabulous Fried Onion Rings

1½ cups all purpose flour

1½ cups beer, active or flat, cold
or room temperature

3 very large yellow onions

3 to 4 cups shortening

Combine flour and beer and blend thoroughly using whisk. Cover and allow batter to sit at least 3 hours at room temperature.

Prepare onions: Carefully peel skins without cutting into outside onion layer. Cut onions into ¼-inch slices and further separate the slices into rings. Set aside.

Preheat oven to 200 degrees about 15 minutes before frying begins. Place brown paper bag or paper towels in layers on a flat pan.

Heat enough shortening for 2-inch depth to 375 degrees in 10-inch electric frying pan, or use deep fryer. With metal tongs, dip onions into batter and carefully place in hot fat. Fry rings, turning them over until they have an even golden color. Add shortening as needed.

Place fried rings in prepared pan and keep warm by placing them into preheated oven.

Special Equipment: Electric frying pan or deep fryer

Ratatouille in Roasted Peppers

6 tablespoons plus ⅓ cup olive oil

1 garlic clove, sliced

8 medium sized red, green and/or yellow peppers

1 medium onion, chopped

2 medium zucchini, cut into ¼-inch slices

½ pound mushrooms, sliced ¼-inch thick

¼ teaspoon salt

1 large eggplant (about 1½ pounds) cut into ½-inch cubes

1 14 to 16-ounce jar spaghetti sauce

1 tablespoon sugar

½ teaspoon basil

Parsley sprigs for garnish

Preheat oven to 450 degrees. Sauté garlic in 3 tablespoons olive oil until garlic is lightly browned. Discard garlic. Cut each pepper lengthwise in half. Remove seeds and stems. Brush pepper halves on all sides with oil and garlic mixture.

Arrange pepper halves in large open roasting pan. Roast peppers 30 to 35 minutes (less for yellow peppers) or until skin puckers and peppers are tender, turning occasionally. Cover and refrigerate.

In large Dutch oven or saucepan, sauté onion in 1 tablespoon oil until tender. Remove with slotted spoon to bowl; set aside.

In same saucepan sauté zucchini and mushrooms in 2 more tablespoons oil. Add salt and cook until tender. Add zucchini mixture to bowl with onion.

In same saucepan, cook eggplant until tender in ⅓ cup oil, about 15 minutes. Return onion and zucchini mixture to eggplant. Add spaghetti sauce a little at a time and stir in remaining seasonings.

Continued on next page

Place mixture in large bowl. Cover and refrigerate at least 2 hours.

To serve, arrange pepper halves on large platter. Fill pepper halves with vegetable mixture. Garnish with parsley sprigs.

Serves: 14 to 16
Special Equipment: Dutch oven, optional

This must be prepared at least 3 hours ahead.

Summer Squash Casserole

1 pound yellow squash, cut in
 ¼-inch slices

⅓ cup onion, chopped

3 tablespoons green pepper,
 chopped

1 2-ounce jar pimento, drained
 and diced

⅓ cup cheddar cheese, grated

1 egg, beaten

¼ teaspoon salt

⅛ teaspoon pepper

1 tablespoon butter

2 tablespoons bread crumbs

Parsley

Dash of paprika

Steam squash and onion for 5 minutes until tender and crisp.

Combine squash mixture with green pepper, pimento, cheese, egg, salt, and pepper. Stir gently. Spoon into buttered 1 quart baking dish.

Combine bread crumbs, parsley, and paprika. Stir well. Sprinkle over squash mixture. Bake at 350 degrees for 25 to 30 minutes.

Serves: 6

An attractive, simple dish — wonderful with summer meals.

Squash Tomato Bake

3 cups prepared spaghetti sauce
2 large or 4 small zucchini, sliced
1 cup grated Parmesan cheese
1 large onion, sliced

4 large tomatoes, sliced
1 large or 2 small yellow summer squash, sliced

Cover bottom of deep baking dish with ½ cup spaghetti sauce. Layer zucchini in bottom of dish. Sprinkle with half of Parmesan cheese. Cover cheese with onions. Top with 1 cup spaghetti sauce. Cover sauce with tomatoes. Sprinkle with remaining cheese. Top with layer of yellow squash and cover with 1½ cups spaghetti sauce. Bake, covered at 350 degrees for 1 hour, uncover for the last 15 minutes.

Serves: 8 to 10

Spaghetti Squash Surprise!

1 spaghetti squash
½ stick butter
2 tablespoons brown sugar

¼ teaspoon cinnamon
¼ cup pistachios, shelled
1 orange, peeled and cut up

Cut squash in half, remove seeds. Bake, cut side down on lightly oiled cookie sheet at 350 degrees for about 45 minutes. Gently remove "spaghetti" to bowl, reserving squash shells, and toss with butter, brown sugar, cinnamon, and pistachios. Gently toss with orange. Place filling in squash shells.

Serves: 4

Tomato Cheese Pie

8 or 9-inch pie shell, baked

1½ pounds Gruyère cheese, thinly sliced

Salt and pepper to taste

2 or 3 large tomatoes, cut into ½-inch slices

1 teaspoon dried basil or 1 tablespoon fresh basil, chopped

2 tablespoons Parmesan cheese

2 tablespoons butter, melted

Sprinkle tomato slices with salt and drain in colander for 30 minutes. Preheat oven to 375 degrees.

Layer cheese slices in bottom of prepared pie shell. Place tomato slices on top of cheese layer. Sprinkle with pepper, basil, and Parmesan cheese. Pour melted butter over top. Bake for 25 minutes or until cheese has melted and top of pie is golden. Serve immediately.

Serves: 8

This is a wonderful alternative to quiche!

Broiled Tomatoes

6 large tomatoes, cut in half

¾ cup onion, minced

¼ teaspoon curry powder

½ teaspoon salt

¼ teaspoon sugar

¼ cup butter

2 teaspoons parsley, chopped

Combine onion, curry, salt, and sugar. Top each tomato half with one tablespoon of mixture plus I tablespoon of butter. Broil under medium heat for 8 to 10 minutes. Sprinkle with chopped parsley.

Serves: 6

Cheesy Zucchini

2 medium-sized zucchini, sliced into ¼-inch pieces

2 tablespoons butter or margarine

1 teaspoon Italian seasoning

4 ounces sour cream

1 tablespoon Italian salad dressing

8 ounce package muenster cheese, sliced (or enough slices to cover zucchini)

Preheat oven to 350 degrees.

Slice zucchini and sauté in butter and Italian seasoning until tender. Using a slotted spoon, place zucchini in 1 quart casserole dish. Pour out all but 2 tablespoons of cooking juices. Add sour cream to juices in pan and mix well.

Spread sour cream mixture over zucchini and sprinkle salad dressing on top. Cover with cheese slices. Bake at 350 degrees for 30 to 45 minutes until bubbly and hot. Serve immediately.

Serves: 6 to 8

Zucchini Oreganato

5 or 6 medium-sized zucchini

4 teaspoons garlic salt

4 teaspoons oregano

3 tomatoes, sliced into ¼-inch pieces

1 or 2 onions, sliced

6 slices American cheese

6 slices bacon

Pepper to taste

Quarter zucchini lengthwise and place on bottom of casserole.

Combine garlic salt, oregano, and pepper to taste. Sprinkle zucchini with one third of mixture. Add layer of sliced tomatoes. Sprinkle with second third of seasonings. Add layer of sliced onions and sprinkle with remaining seasonings.

Cover with slices of American cheese and top with slices of uncooked bacon. Bake in 350 degree oven for 45 minutes, or until heated through and cheese has melted.

Serves: 6

Orange Glazed Sweet Potatoes

. . . .

6 medium yams or sweet potatoes
½ cup brown sugar
½ cup granulated sugar
1 tablespoon cornstarch

½ cup orange juice
4 tablespoons butter or margarine
Orange sections, optional

Boil yams in their jackets about 20 minutes until almost tender. Do not overcook. Cool, peel, and cut in thick slices; lay in greased shallow baking dish.

Mix sugars and cornstarch in saucepan. Put over medium heat and add orange juice, stirring constantly for about 5 minutes. Add butter and stir until melted. Pour sauce over potatoes.

Bake at 375 degrees for 25 to 30 minutes. Arrange orange sections on potatoes before baking. Baste with glaze halfway through cooking time.

Serves: 6

. . . .

Holiday Sweet Potatoes

. . . .

2 32-ounce cans yams or sweet
   potatoes
1 stick butter
½ cup light cream
½ cup cream sherry
½ teaspoon cinnamon

½ teaspoon salt
½ teaspoon nutmeg
½ teaspoon ground cloves
1 cup light brown sugar, packed
Chopped walnuts (optional)
Butter pieces as needed

Mash potatoes; add butter, cream, and sherry. Stir in cinnamon, salt, nutmeg, and cloves. Adjust seasonings to taste. Place into a 9×13-inch baking dish. Sprinkle brown sugar over mixture. Top with nuts and dot with butter. Bake at 350 degrees for 25 to 30 minutes.

Serves: 12

Garlic Potatoes

. . . .

1½ pounds potatoes, peeled and
   boiled
½ teaspoon salt
Pepper to taste

12 ounces sharp cheddar cheese,
   grated
⅔ cup heavy cream
4 cloves garlic, minced

Thinly slice potatoes into ⅛-inch circles, place in buttered baking dish. Sprinkle with salt and pepper. Sprinkle 4 ounces grated cheese over top. Slowly pour ⅓ cup heavy cream over cheese. Put another 4 ounces cheese on top. Pour rest of cream over cheese. Top with remaining cheese and minced garlic. Bake at 350 degrees for 40 minutes.

Serves: 6

. . . .

Grandma's Potato Pie

5 pounds potatoes

½ pound butter, cut into small pieces

½ teaspoon salt

½ teaspoon pepper

2 eggs

2 cups hot milk

⅔ cup Parmesan cheese, grated

½ pound prosciutto, diced

¾ pound mozzarella cheese, diced

½ cup bread crumbs, toasted

Preheat oven to 325 degrees.

Peel, quarter and boil potatoes until done. Drain. Add next six ingredients to potatoes and whip at medium speed until mixture is smooth. Add prosciutto and mozzarella cheese and blend.

Press bread crumbs into sides of one large glass pie pan or two small pans. Reserve two tablespoons of crumbs for garnish. Pour potato mixture into prepared pan. Sprinkle reserved bread crumbs on top.

Bake for 40 minutes.

Serves: 6 to 8

This is easily halved.

Potatoes Byron

. . . .

6 large baking potatoes
¼ pound butter, melted
½ teaspoon salt
Pepper to taste

Sherry (optional)
¾ pound Swiss cheese, shredded
½ cup heavy cream

Bake potatoes. Peel potatoes and break up coarsely. Add butter, salt, pepper, and sherry. Turn into glass baking dish, sprinkle with cheese and cream. Bake at 375 degrees for 20 minutes or until cheese melts and makes golden crust.

Serves: 6

Green Rice

. . . .

1 cup uncooked rice
2 cups boiling water
10 ounces sharp cheddar cheese, grated
1 teaspoon salt (optional)
2 cups milk
2 eggs, beaten
¼ cup salad oil

2 small onions, diced
½ bunch parsley, chopped
Tops, stems and leaves from ½ bunch of celery
¼ teaspoon sage
¼ teaspoon tarragon
¼ teaspoon basil

Cook rice in 2 cups boiling water, until all water is absorbed; rice must be tender. Combine remaining ingredients in order listed and add to rice. Mix well. Put into greased casserole dish. Bake at 350 degrees for 1½ hours.

Serves: 4 to 6

. . . .

Three Cheese Baked Rice

3 tablespoons butter
1 small onion, chopped
1 small red pepper, diced
1 small green pepper, diced
1 rib celery, diced
1 cup uncooked rice
1¾ cups chicken broth

¾ cup white wine
1 small green chili pepper, diced
¾ teaspoon salt
1½ cups sour cream
2½ ounces Gruyère cheese
2½ ounces cheddar cheese
2½ ounces mozzarella cheese

Preheat oven to 350 degrees.

In Dutch oven or oven-safe pan sauté onion, peppers, and celery in butter for 3 minutes. Add rice, chicken broth, wine, chili pepper, and salt. Bring to boil, cover and place in oven. Bake 15 to 20 minutes or until all liquid has been absorbed. Remove from oven and transfer to large bowl. Let cool slightly.

Stir sour cream and cheeses into cooled rice mixture and transfer to a buttered 13×9-inch pan. Bake at 400 degrees for 20 minutes or until lightly browned.

Serves: 6 to 10
Special Equipment: Dutch oven or oven-safe pan

Risotto Primavera

3½ ounces small asparagus spears

3½ ounces zucchini

¼ cup green peas, frozen

½ cup butter

½ cup onion, chopped

1 cup uncooked rice

6 cups chicken broth

⅓ cup mushrooms, sautéed and chopped

1 green pepper, roasted, peeled and diced

1¼ cups tomatoes, peeled, seeded and diced

6 tablespoons Parmesan cheese

Wash and trim asparagus, zucchini, and peas and boil separately until tender. Drain. Dice asparagus and zucchini.

In large pan sauté onion in ¼ cup butter until lightly brown. Add rice and stir a few minutes so that all grains are well coated. Add broth gradually and bring mixture to a simmer, stirring constantly. Cook for about 8 minutes more. Add asparagus, zucchini, peas, mushrooms, peppers, and tomatoes and bring to a simmer again. Cook until rice is tender.

Spoon rice into heated serving dish, add ¼ cup butter and Parmesan. Stir until butter and cheese are melted. Serve immediately.

Serves: 6 to 8

Herbed Rice

. . . .

1 stick margarine
1 cup uncooked rice
1 cup onion, chopped
½ teaspoon summer savory
¼ teaspoon salt
1 teaspoon rosemary

½ teaspoon marjoram
1 cup mushrooms, sliced
3 chicken bouillon cubes dissolved in 2 cups boiling water

In large skillet, melt margarine. Sauté rice and onions until onions are translucent. Add summer savory, salt, rosemary, and marjoram to rice mixture. Add mushrooms, dissolved bouillon cubes and water to rice and stir well. Cover and simmer for 20 minutes or until water is absorbed.

Serves: 6 to 8

Pineapple Casserole

. . . .

4 eggs, beaten
2 tablespoons flour
¾ cup sugar
1 20-ounce can crushed pineapple

3 slices crumbled bread, crusts removed
½ stick butter, melted

Combine eggs, flour, sugar and pineapple. Place in 1½ quart buttered casserole dish. Sprinkle with bread crumbs and pour melted butter over top. Bake at 350 degrees for 1 hour.

Serves: 4 to 6

An unusual accompaniment for ham or pork chops.

Hot Fruit Casserole

. . . .

1 16-ounce can sliced pineapple
1 16-ounce can peach halves
1 16-ounce can pear halves
1 16-ounce can apricot halves
1 16-ounce can pitted cherries

2 tablespoons flour
½ cup brown sugar
1 stick butter
1 cup sherry

Drain all fruit. Arrange in alternate layers in deep casserole.

In top of double boiler combine: flour, brown sugar, butter, and sherry. Cook, stirring, until smooth and thickened. Pour over fruit and cover. Let stand in refrigerator overnight or all day.

Just before serving, bake at 350 degrees until hot and bubbly, about 20 to 25 minutes.

Serves: 8
Special Equipment: Double boiler

Save calories by using fruit canned in unsweetened syrup.

Phipps Estate at Old Westbury

Desserts

"Sweet Victory"

"Bountiful" is a word sometimes used to describe Long Island and, indeed, we truly enjoy a wealth of recreational, educational, cultural, and commercial benefits. The Island "wealth" that is usually the most interesting to observers, however, is that which one can total in a bank book.

In the early 1900s, men who earned millions in Manhattan began to look for a place to get away from it all. The Island offered the perfect choice for many of them. Easily accessible by road, rail or boat, the rolling, wooded countryside was perfect for bridle paths, hunting preserves and golf courses, while the center plains were just right for race tracks and polo fields. Yachtsmen appreciated the many protected harbors, and the fine climate encouraged establishment of English-style formal gardens.

The Guggenheims, Mackays, Pratts, Whitneys, Vanderbilts, Roosevelts, Phippses, Woolworths, Marshall Fields, and J.P. Morgans are only a few of the families who lived and played on the Island. By 1920, almost 600 estates, ranging in size from fifty to 1,750 acres, existed virtually side by side along the North Shore from Great Neck to Northport. This 110-square mile area, dubbed "The Gold Coast," represented less than ten percent of Long Island. Many of the mansions built on these estates were primarily for vacationing and entertaining and frequently contained as many as 100 rooms and thirty baths.

Some of the mansions have survived and are open to the public today. A few that offer tours are the former Phipps estate at Old Westbury Gardens, the Sands Point homes of the Guggenheims, William K. Vanderbilt's "summer place" at Centerport, and the "Summer White House" at Sagamore Hill, built by our twenty-fifth president, Theodore Roosevelt.

Chocolate Raspberry Cake

12½ ounces semisweet chocolate

2½ ounces unsweetened chocolate

2 sticks butter

Scant ½ cup raspberry jam

10 eggs, separated

⅞ cup sugar

1 cup cake flour

Chocolate Sauce:

12 ounces semisweet chocolate

¼ cup butter

Raspberry jam (optional)

Whipped cream (optional)

Preheat oven to 350 degrees. Butter and flour two 8-inch cake pans.

In a medium saucepan, combine chocolate, butter, and jam over low heat until chocolate is melted. Add half the sugar to the yolks, beat until pale yellow.

Combine the rest of the sugar with the whites and beat whites until they form soft peaks.

Combine chocolate with yolk mixture, sift in cake flour and fold in whites. Pour into cake pans. Bake at 350 degrees for 25 minutes or until cake is firm and springy to the touch. Spread raspberry jam between layers if desired.

Melt chocolate with butter over low heat, stirring constantly. Pour chocolate sauce onto finished cake and turn cake to let chocolate drip down sides of cake. Serve with whipped cream if desired.

Serves: 12

Marquis de Chocolate

8 ounces semisweet chocolate

6 eggs separated, room temperature

Pinch of salt

1 cup sugar

1 tablespoon vanilla

½ pound butter, room temperature

2 packages lady fingers

Toasted almonds to cover, optional

Melt chocolate in a double boiler.

Beat egg whites with salt until stiff. Gradually beat sugar into egg whites until all is incorporated and mixture becomes shiny. Add hot melted chocolate to the egg white mixture slowly.

In a separate bowl beat egg yolks, vanilla, and softened butter until consistency of cream. Mix egg yolk mixture into egg white mixture.

On a flat plate or cake dish, alternate lady fingers and filling, ending with filling. Spread filling to cover sides and top as a frosting. Cover with toasted almonds if desired. Chill until serving.

Serves: 10
Special Equipment: Double boiler

This is a glamourous dessert!

Chocolate Chip Coffee Cake

Batter:

3 cups flour

2 cups sugar

2 teaspoons baking soda

3 teaspoons baking powder

½ pound butter, room
temperature

4 eggs

16 ounces sour cream

2 teaspoons vanilla

Chip mix:

12 ounces chocolate chips

½ cup sugar

1 teaspoon cinnamon

Preheat oven to 350 degrees. Sift dry batter ingredients together into a bowl. In a separate bowl, cream butter. Add eggs one at a time. Stir in sour cream and vanilla. Slowly beat dry ingredients into butter mixture. Pour half of batter ingredients into a greased lasagna pan.

Mix chocolate chips, sugar, and cinnamon in a separate bowl. Sprinkle half of chip mix on batter in pan. Pour remaining half of batter on chips and top with rest of chip mix. Bake for 45 minutes to 1 hour. Cool before cutting.

Serves: 8 to 10

French Chocolate Cake

. . . .

20 ounces semisweet chocolate,
  coarsely chopped
1 cup unsalted butter
¼ cup brandy
6 eggs separated, room
  temperature

1 cup sugar
¼ cup sifted all purpose flour
1 teaspoon vanilla extract
¼ cup walnuts, coarsely chopped
½ cup whipping cream

Preheat oven to 350 degrees. Butter and flour two 9-inch round cake pans or a springform pan.

Melt 12 ounces of chocolate with butter and brandy in double boiler over simmering water. Stir until smooth. Remove chocolate mixture from top of double boiler and cool completely.

Beat egg yolks with electric mixer until pale yellow and ribbon forms when beaters are lifted. Gradually add sugar, flour, vanilla and continue to beat until thick.

Using clean, dry beaters, beat egg whites in another bowl until stiff peaks form.

Fold melted chocolate in with yolk mixture. Gently fold in ¼ of egg whites. Fold in remaining egg whites. Fold in nuts. Pour batter into prepared pans.

Bake until tester inserted in centers comes out clean, about 30 minutes. Cool in pans on rack, about 10 minutes. Invert onto racks, cool completely.

Continued on next page

. . . .

Melt remaining chocolate in double boiler over simmering water. Add heated cream and stir until smooth. Transfer to bowl set over larger bowl filled with ice. Using electric mixer, beat until cool.

For layer cake, set one cake layer on plate, spread on ⅓ icing, top with second cake layer. Cover top and sides of cake with remaining icing.

For springform pan, spread icing on tops and sides.

Chill at least 1 hour before serving.

Serves: 12
Special Equipment: Double boiler

Black Bottom Cupcakes

Cake:
1½ cups flour

1 cup sugar

¼ cup cocoa powder, unsweetened

1 teaspoon baking soda

½ teaspoon salt

1 cup water

⅓ cup oil

1 teaspoon vanilla

1 teaspoon white vinegar

Filling:
8 ounce package cream cheese, softened

1 egg

⅓ cup sugar

⅛ teaspoon salt

Topping:
6 ounces mini chocolate chips

Preheat oven to 350 degrees. Line cupcake pan with paper or foil liners.

Sift dry cake ingredients together into a bowl. Add liquid cake ingredients and stir well. Fill each cupcake paper liner ½ full.

Combine filling ingredients. Drop 1 teaspoon of filling on top of each cupcake. Sprinkle with mini chips.

Bake 15 to 18 minutes or until cream cheese filling is set.

Yield: 12 large or 4 dozen small cupcakes

A fun dessert to take on a picnic.

Hazelnut Cheesecake

1½ cups graham cracker crumbs
¼ cup sugar
½ stick butter, melted
27 ounces cream cheese
1 cup sugar
1 cup hazelnuts, ground and toasted
4 eggs, room temperature

1 egg yolk
½ teaspoon lemon juice
½ teaspoon vanilla
¼ teaspoon almond extract
Pinch of salt
2 tablespoons plus 1 teaspoon cornstarch
1 cup half and half

Mix graham crackers, ¼ cup sugar, and melted butter. Put in bottom of 10-inch springform pan. Bake at 350 degrees for 10 to 12 minutes. Cool to room temperature.

Using hand mixer beat cream cheese and sugar together until smooth and light. Mix in nuts, eggs, egg yolk, lemon juice, vanilla, almond extract, and salt.

In a separate bowl dissolve corn starch into half and half. Add cornstarch mixture to cream cheese mixture. Mix well. Pour filling into crust.

Place cake pan in large roasting pan. Add enough boiling water to go halfway up sides of cake pan. Bake approximately 1 hour at 350 degrees until lightly brown and cake pulls away from sides of pan. Cool on rack and refrigerate at least 4 hours before serving.

Serves: 10 to 12
Special Equipment: Springform pan

Blueberry Cobbler

4 cups blueberries

2 cups sugar

1 cup all-purpose flour

1 teaspoon double-acting baking powder

½ teaspoon cinnamon

¼ teaspoon mace

¼ teaspoon salt

2 teaspoons lemon zest

1 cup milk

½ teaspoon vanilla

½ cup unsalted butter, melted and cooled

Rinse and pick over berries. Mix fruit and 1 cup sugar in a bowl and let stand for 30 minutes.

In another bowl sift together 1 cup sugar, flour, baking powder, cinnamon, mace, and salt. Add lemon zest and mix. Add milk and vanilla and stir until combined.

Pour melted butter into a 10-inch square baking pan. Add batter, stirring to combine it with the butter. Spoon fruit over the mixture. Bake in preheated 350 degree oven for 30 minutes. Bake 10 to 15 minutes longer at 400 degrees, or until golden brown around edges. Let cobbler cool for 20 minutes.

Serve with vanilla ice cream.

Serves: 6 to 8

Other seasonal fruits may be used in place of or combined with the blueberries.

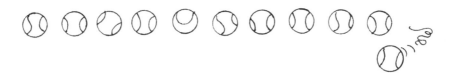

German Apple Cake

5 baking apples peeled, cored, and thinly sliced

2 teaspoons ground cinnamon

5 tablespoons sugar

3 cups unsifted flour

2½ cups sugar

½ teaspoon salt

1½ teaspoons baking soda

1½ teaspoons baking powder

4 eggs

1 cup vegetable oil

2 teaspoons vanilla extract

⅓ cup orange juice

Glaze:

1½ cups confectioners sugar

2 tablespoons butter or margarine, softened

1½ teaspoons vanilla extract

1 to 2 tablespoons water

Grease and flour 10-inch tube or bundt pan. Preheat oven to 350 degrees. Combine apples with cinnamon and 5 tablespoons of sugar.

Sift flour, sugar, salt, baking soda and baking powder together into a large bowl. Add eggs, oil, vanilla, and orange juice. Blend on low speed for 1 minute with an electric mixer. Scrape sides of bowl, increase speed and blend for 3 minutes until batter is thick.

Fill pan with alternate layers of batter and apples, beginning and ending with batter. Bake 1½ to 1¾ hours or until cake tester inserted in center comes out clean. Cool cake on rack for 10 minutes. Invert cake and remove pan. Allow cake to cool completely before glazing.

Glaze: Mix confectioners sugar, soft butter, vanilla, and water until smooth. Drizzle on cooled cake.

Serves: 10 to 12

Special Equipment: Bundt pan

Great fall dessert.

Carrot Cake

2 cups flour

2 cups sugar

2 teaspoons baking soda

2 teaspoons cinnamon

1½ cups salad oil

4 eggs

3 cups carrots, grated

1 cup nuts, chopped

Icing (optional):

8 ounce package cream cheese, softened

1 stick butter or margarine, softened

1 pound confectioners sugar

2 teaspoons vanilla

Sift dry ingredients together. Add oil and stir well. Add eggs one at a time. Mix well after each. Add carrots and nuts and blend.

Bake at 350 degrees in 2 greased and floured 9-inch cake pans or in 1 angel food cake pan for about 25 minutes or until tester inserted comes out clean.

Icing: Cream butter and cheese together. Add sugar and vanilla. Spread generously over cake.

Serves: 8

Special Equipment: Food Processor (optional)

Food processor makes short work of grating carrots.

Cream Cheese Pound Cake

½ pound butter

8 ounces cream cheese

6 eggs

1¾ cups sugar

2 cups cake flour

1 teaspoon vanilla

Cream butter and cream cheese together. Add eggs one at a time. Add sugar, flour, and vanilla. Combine thoroughly. Pour mixture into angel food cake pan. Bake at 325 degrees for 1 hour or until done. Leave in pan 10 to 15 minutes before removing.

Serves: 10

Special Equipment: Angel food cake pan

Sinfully good with Caramel Sauce on page 251.

Mace Cake

1 cup butter

1¾ cups sugar

2 teaspoons mace

5 eggs

2 cups flour, sifted

Confectioners sugar

Cream butter with sugar. Add mace, and stir. Add eggs one at a time, beating batter after each one. Mix in flour. Combine thoroughly.

Grease and flour bundt pan. Pour in batter. Bake at 325 degrees for 1½ hours. Cool about 10 minutes before turning out. Sprinkle with confectioners sugar before serving.

Serves: 8 to 10

Special Equipment: Bundt pan

Graham Cracker Cake

2 cups sugar

½ pound margarine or butter, room temperature

5 eggs

3 cups graham cracker crumbs, packed

¾ cup milk

7 ounce can grated coconut

1 cup pecans, chopped

Juice from one small can crushed pineapple

Frosting:

1 stick butter or margarine, room temperature

8 ounces cream cheese, room temperature

1 pound confectioners sugar

1 teaspoon vanilla

Mix sugar and margarine well, add eggs and mix. Add crumbs, milk, coconut, and pecans. Mix well.

Generously grease and flour two 9-inch layer pans. Bake at 350 degrees for 40 to 50 minutes. Spoon pineapple juice over cooled layers.

Frosting: Cream butter and cream cheese together. Mix in sugar. Add vanilla and stir well. Frost cake and refrigerate.

Serves: 8 to 10

French Silk Chocolate Pie

½ cup butter, room temperature

¾ cup extrafine granulated sugar

2 ounces unsweetened chocolate, melted

1 teaspoon vanilla extract

¼ teaspoon almond extract, optional

2 large eggs

Baked and cooled 8-inch pie shell

Whipped cream

Chopped toasted almonds or shaved chocolate

Cream butter thoroughly. Add sugar gradually and continue beating for 4 to 5 minutes. Blend in melted, cooled chocolate, add vanilla and almond extract.

At medium speed on electric mixer, add eggs, one at a time, beating for 5 minutes after each. Turn mixture into cooled pie shell and chill several hours.

Garnish with whipped cream and sprinkle with nuts or curls of shaved chocolate.

Serves: 6 to 8

Also makes a lovely filling for large or small cream puffs, served with a drizzle of chocolate sauce.

Chocolate Cheese Torte

Crust:
1⅓ cups graham cracker crumbs

3 tablespoons sugar

3 tablespoons unsweetened cocoa powder

⅓ cup butter or margarine, melted

Filling:
4 3-ounce packages cream cheese

¾ cup sugar

2 eggs

1 tablespoon coffee flavored liqueur or rum

1 teaspoon vanilla

First Frosting:
8 ounces sour cream

1 square unsweetened chocolate, grated

Second Frosting:
1½ teaspoons instant coffee powder

2 tablespoons boiling water

4 squares semi-sweet chocolate

4 egg yolks

⅓ cup sugar

1 tablespoon coffee flavored liqueur or rum

½ teaspoon vanilla

4 egg whites

½ cup heavy cream, whipped

Crust: Blend crumbs, 3 tablespoons sugar, cocoa, and butter until well mixed. Press firmly onto the bottom and sides of 9-inch springform pan. Bake at 350 degrees for 10 minutes. Let cool while preparing filling.

Continued on next page

Filling: Beat cream cheese in a large bowl with electric mixer at high speed until light and fluffy. Gradually beat in ¾ cup sugar. Add eggs one at a time, beating well after each addition. Add 1 tablespoon liqueur and 1 teaspoon vanilla. Turn into baked crust. Bake at 350 degrees for 30 minutes. Cool for 10 minutes on a wire rack.

First Frosting: Gently spread sour cream over baked layer. Sprinkle with grated chocolate. Refrigerate.

Second Frosting: Dissolve coffee in boiling water in top of a double boiler over hot, not boiling, water. Add chocolate. Stir until melted and blended.

Beat 4 egg yolks in medium size bowl with electric mixer until thick. Gradually beat in ⅓ cup sugar. Add small amount of chocolate mixture. Beat well. Continue adding small amounts of chocolate mixture to egg mixture and beating until all has been added. Add remaining liqueur and vanilla.

Beat egg whites until stiff. Gently fold into chocolate mixture. Spread over cool baked layer. Refrigerate until firm. When ready to serve: loosen side of pan, remove. Place cake on serving plate. Decorate with whipped cream when ready to serve.

Serves: 10
Special Equipment: Double boiler/Springform pan

Apple Cream Pie

9-inch pie crust, unbaked
4 medium cooking apples, peeled
   and thinly sliced
1 cup whipping cream
1 cup sugar
1 egg, beaten

3 tablespoons flour
1 teaspoon cinnamon
1 teaspoon vanilla
¼ teaspoon nutmeg
⅛ teaspoon salt
½ cup pecans, chopped

Preheat oven to 450 degrees. Line uncooked pie shell with apples.

Mix together cream, sugar, egg, flour, cinnamon, vanilla, nutmeg, and salt, stirring well after each ingredient is added. Pour over apple slices. Bake at 450 degrees for 10 minutes, then sprinkle top with chopped nuts.

Reduce heat to 350 degrees. Bake until apples are tender, 40 to 45 minutes longer.

Serves: 6

Rainbow Tart

Pâté Sucre:

1¼ cups flour

1 tablespoon sugar

½ cup toasted crushed hazelnuts, almonds, or walnuts

Pinch of salt

¼ pound sweet butter, room temperature

1 to 2 tablespoons water

Filling:

¼ pound sweet butter, room temperature

¾ cup sugar

8 ounces cream cheese, room temperature

1 teaspoon vanilla

2 eggs

Topping:

1 pint strawberries

3 large kiwis

1 large navel orange

¼ cup apricot jam

1 tablespoon rum

Mint sprigs for garnish

Pâté Sucre: Combine dry ingredients, cut in butter to coarse cornmeal stage. Add enough water to make pastry stick together. Roll out pastry to fit 9-inch pie pan or individual tart shells. Weigh down with rice or beans. Bake at 350 degrees for 10 to 15 minutes until lightly browned. Cool.

Filling: Cream butter and sugar on low speed until fluffy. Add cream cheese; beat at medium speed until smooth. Beat in vanilla, then eggs, one at a time. Fill tart shell. Bake at 350 degrees for 20 to 30 minutes until filling is set and lightly brown. Cool.

Topping: Slice fruits and arrange decoratively over filling. Heat apricot jam with rum. Simmer for 5 to 7 minutes. Brush over tart. Garnish with mint sprigs.

Serves: 8

Lime Pie

1 cup sugar
3 tablespoons cornstarch
¼ cup butter
1 tablespoon lime rind, grated
¼ cup lime juice
3 unbeaten egg yolks

1 cup milk
1 cup sour cream
9-inch pie shell, baked
1 cup heavy cream, whipped
Lime, thinly sliced for garnish

Combine sugar and cornstarch in sauce pan. Add butter, lime rind, lime juice, and egg yolks. Stir in milk. Cook over medium heat, stirring constantly until thickened. Cool. Fold in sour cream and pour mixture into baked pie shell. Cover with whipped cream. Chill for 2 hours. Garnish with thin slices of lime before serving.

Serves: 6

Super summer fare!

Peach Pie

Pastry for 2 pie crusts, top and bottom

8 to 9 large, ripe peaches, peeled, halved and pitted

1½ teaspoons lemon juice

9 tablespoons brown sugar

9 teaspoons bourbon

2 teaspoons cinnamon

3 tablespoons butter or margarine

Preheat oven to 350 degrees.

Place peach halves face-up in pie shells. Sprinkle each pie with ¾ teaspoon lemon juice. Into each peach half, put ½ tablespoon brown sugar and ½ teaspoon bourbon. Sprinkle each pie with a teaspoon of cinnamon. Dot each pie with 1½ tablespoons of butter.

Cover with top crusts and bake at 350 degrees for 40 to 45 minutes. Allow to cool slightly and serve.

Yield: 2 pies

Cranberry Pie

· ·

Crust:
2 ounces hazelnuts

1¾ cups flour

½ cup confectioners sugar

½ teaspoon lemon zest, grated

½ teaspoon cinnamon

½ cup sweet butter, cut in bits

1 large egg, lightly beaten

Filling:
12 ounces cranberries

1 cup granulated sugar

¼ cup water

Preheat oven to 375 degrees.

Crust: Toast hazelnuts 8 to 10 minutes in oven, rub in clean kitchen towel to remove skins. Cool completely. Process in blender or food processor until finely ground. Measure out ½ cup for crust.

Process nuts, flour, sugar, lemon zest, and cinnamon in food processor about 8 to 10 seconds. Add butter bits and mix until it resembles coarse crumbs. Set aside 1½ tablespoons egg. Drizzle remaining egg over pastry and mix until gathered into a ball. Shape dough into thin disk, refrigerate wrapped in plastic wrap for 30 minutes.

Filling: Heat cranberries, sugar, and water in saucepan. Bring to a boil stirring constantly over high heat until very thick, about 5 minutes. Cool completely. Reheat oven to 375 degrees.

Continued on next page

· ·

Remove pastry from refrigerator. Roll out ⅔ pastry into 12-inch circle on wax paper or pastry cloth. Press into bottom and up the sides of 9-inch springform pan. Roll remaining ⅓ pastry into 9 to 10-inch circle, cut into ten ½-inch wide strips for lattice top. Freeze strips on baking sheet 3 to 5 minutes before handling. Spoon cooled filling into pastry crust. Smooth top.

Lift pastry lattice strips with knife. Arrange 1½ inches apart in lattice pattern on top of filling. Press remaining 3 strips around edge, trim, and crimp. Run a thin metal spatula around edge of pie to keep pastry from sticking to pan. Brush with remaining egg.

Bake for 40 to 45 minutes until pastry is golden brown. Cool on wire rack 10 to 20 minutes. Remove from pan, cool completely before serving.

Yield: 1 pie
Special Equipment: Food Processor/Springform pan/Blender

Baklava

· ·

1 pound frozen phyllo leaves (strudel pastry)	1½ teaspoons cinnamon
1 pound butter	1 cup honey
1 pound walnut meats	1 cup water
	⅔ cup sugar

Thaw pastry following package directions. After removing from sealed plastic bag keep covered with wax paper and damp cloth while constructing this recipe. Phyllo dries out very quickly.

Clarify butter: Melt over low heat without stirring. Use only clarified (clear yellow) butter. Reserve milky white residue for other uses or discard it.

Line a 12"×15" broiler pan with heavy duty aluminum foil. Brush foil with butter. Use a food processor to finely chop walnuts. Stir in cinnamon. Preheat oven to 325 degrees.

Use first third of the phyllo sheets and place 1 sheet at a time in buttered pan. Brush each sheet well with clarified butter. Continue stacking phyllo sheets until all are used. Spread half of the chopped walnut mixture over the stacked phyllo.

Layer and butter the second third of phyllo sheets. Spread remaining nuts on phyllo. Continue layering and buttering the remaining phyllo sheets. If there is any butter left, pour it on top.

Continued on next page

· ·

Cut 2-inch squares, rectangles or diamond shapes through pastry to bottom of lower sheet being careful not to cut aluminum foil. Bake about 45 minutes until pastry is brown and crisp.

While pastry is baking, combine honey, water, and sugar in medium sauce pan. Cook until syrup comes to a boil. Remove from heat and cool to room temperature.

When phyllo is finished baking, immediately pour syrup over hot pastry. Let stand a day before serving. This pastry requires no refrigeration.

Yield: 42 to 48 diamonds
Special Equipment: Food Processor

Well worth the effort.

Pecan Tarts

. . . .

Tart shell:

½ cup margarine, melted

½ cup granulated sugar

2 egg yolks

1 teaspoon almond extract

2 cups sifted flour

Filling:

½ cup margarine

½ cup dark corn syrup

1 cup confectioners sugar

1 cup pecans, chopped

3 to 4 dozen pecan halves

Mix melted margarine, sugar, egg yolks, and almond extract. Slowly stir in flour. Press firmly into miniature cupcake tins. Bake at 400 degrees for 8 to 10 minutes. Remove from oven and cool. Reduce oven temperature to 350 degrees.

Bring margarine, dark corn syrup, and confectioners sugar to a boil. Stir in chopped pecans. Spoon into shells and top each shell with pecan halves. Bake at 350 degrees for 5 minutes. Remove from tin while warm.

Yield: 3 Dozen

Special Equipment: Mini cupcake tins

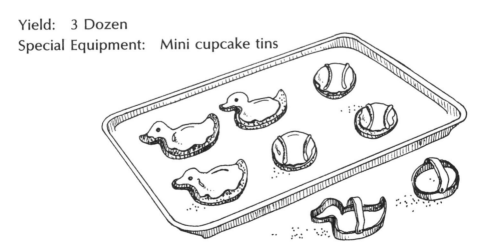

. . . .

Chocolate Fudge Cookies

2 cups (12 ounces) semisweet
   chocolate morsels

4 tablespoons sweet butter

1 14-ounce-can sweetened
   condensed milk

1 teaspoon vanilla

1 cup flour

1 cup pecans, broken into large
   pieces

Preheat oven to 350 degrees. Line cookie sheets with foil, shiny side up.

Place chocolate morsels and butter in top of large double boiler over warm water on moderate heat. Stir occasionally until melted and smooth. Remove top of double boiler from heat. Stir in condensed milk and vanilla, then flour, then pecans.

Using a rounded teaspoon of mixture for each cookie, place 1 to 2 inches apart on foil. Bake exactly 7 minutes. Cookies will feel soft but will become firmer when cooled. When cool, use a wide spatula to transfer cookies to rack.

Yield: 4 Dozen
Special Equipment: Double boiler

A chocolate lover's delight.

Cowboy Cookies

. . . .

1 cup oil
1 cup brown sugar
1 cup granulated sugar
2 eggs
2 cups flour
1 teaspoon baking soda

½ teaspoon baking powder
½ teaspoon salt
2 cups (12 ounces) chocolate
  chips
2 cups oatmeal

Preheat oven to 350 degrees. Beat oil and sugars together. Add eggs and beat. Sift dry ingredients together and add to egg mixture. Add chocolate chips and oatmeal and mix. Drop heaping teaspoons onto greased cookie sheet. Bake for 15 minutes or until golden brown.

Yield: 9 Dozen

For more nutrition, substitute ½ cup wheat germ for ½ cup flour.

White Chocolate Chunk and Macadamia Nut Cookies

. . . .

⅔ cup sweet butter
½ cup granulated sugar
⅓ cup brown sugar
1 large egg
1 teaspoon vanilla

1½ cups flour
3½ ounces macadamia nuts,
  chopped
6 ounces white chocolate chunks

Preheat oven to 325 degrees. Grease 2 cookie sheets.

With an electric mixer beat butter, sugars, egg, and vanilla until fluffy. Add flour and beat until well mixed. Fold in nuts and white chocolate. Drop heaping teaspoons onto cookie sheet and bake approximately 15 minutes.

Yield: 2½ dozen

. . . .

Forgotten Cookies

2 eggs whites, room temperature
¾ cup granulated sugar
½ teaspoon vanilla
6 ounce package semi-sweet
   chocolate bits

1 cup nuts, pecans or walnuts,
   chopped

Preheat oven to 350 degrees. Center oven rack to accommodate cookie sheets. Line cookie sheets with foil.

Beat egg whites until stiff but not dry. Beat in sugar gradually. Beat in vanilla. Fold in chocolate bits and chopped nuts.

Drop heaping teaspoons on foil lined sheets. Put cookie sheets in preheated oven, quickly close door, and immediately turn off oven heat. Leave undisturbed for 8 hours or overnight. Do not open oven door until time is up.

Yield: 2 Dozen

Shortbread Cookies

1 pound butter
1 cup extra fine sugar
1 cup cornstarch

4 cups flour
Confectioners sugar

Cream butter and sugar together. Add cornstarch. Add the flour a little at a time (you'll need to use your hands to mix when all the flour has been added). Press into an 11×16 cookie sheet or jelly roll pan. Prick all over with a fork. Bake at 350 degrees approximately 30 minutes, until lightly browned.

Cut into rectangles while warm. Sprinkle with confectioners sugar before serving.

Yield: 5 to 6 Dozen

Molasses Sugar Cookies

¾ cup margarine or butter
1 cup sugar
¼ cup molasses
1 egg
2 cups flour

2 teaspoons baking soda
½ teaspoon ground cloves
½ teaspoon ground ginger
1 teaspoon ground cinnamon
½ teaspoon salt

Melt margarine or butter in 3 quart sauce pan, cool. Add sugar, molasses, and egg. Mix well with a wooden spoon. Sift the remaining ingredients together and add to butter mixture. Stir with spoon, do not use a mixer. Cover and chill 3 to 4 hours.

Form into 1-inch balls, roll in sugar and place on greased cookie sheet 2 inches apart. Bake at 375 degrees for 8 to 10 minutes.

Yield: 3 Dozen

Pecan Crescent Cookies

½ pound butter, room
   temperature

5 tablespoons sugar

2 teaspoons vanilla

1 tablespoon water

2 cups flour

½ teaspoon salt

2 cups (8 ounces) pecans,
   chopped

Confectioners sugar

Cream butter and add sugar, vanilla, and water. Sift flour and salt together. Stir into butter mixture. Add pecans and mix thoroughly. Using a portion about the size of a walnut, form into a crescent shape.

Bake at 325 degrees for 20 minutes or until lightly browned. Sprinkle with confectioners sugar while warm.

Yield: 40 to 50 Cookies

Date Torte Bars

¼ pound butter or margarine

1 cup brown sugar

2 eggs, slightly beaten

¾ cup flour

½ cup nuts, chopped

½ cup dates, chopped

1 teaspoon vanilla

½ teaspoon baking soda

¼ teaspoon salt

Confectioners sugar

Melt butter in 8 or 9-inch baking pan. Remove from heat. Add remaining ingredients to pan one at a time and beat with fork until mixture is smooth and creamy. Bake at 350 degrees for 35 minutes.

Cut into bars. Sprinkle with confectioners sugar if desired.

Serves: 10

Chocolate Mint Brownies

Bottom layer:

1 cup sugar

½ cup butter or margarine, room
temperature

4 eggs, beaten

1 cup flour

½ teaspoon salt

1 16-ounce can chocolate syrup

1 teaspoon vanilla

Middle layer:

2 cups confectioners sugar

½ cup butter, room temperature

3 tablespoons crème de menthe
liqueur

Glaze:

1 cup chocolate chips (6 ounces)

6 tablespoons butter

Cream sugar and butter together. Add eggs, one at a time. Then add
flour, salt, chocolate syrup and vanilla. Mix well. Place in greased
9×13-inch pan. Bake at 350 degrees for 30 minutes. Cool.

Cream sugar and butter. Add crème de menthe and spread over
cooled cake.

Melt chocolate chips and butter together over low heat. Spread
"glaze" over cake. Chill and cut into 2-inch squares.

Yield: 25 brownies

*Great for any "green" holiday such as St. Patrick's Day, Christmas or
Easter.*

Light Pralines

3 cups sugar
1 cup evaporated milk
¾ cup white corn syrup
4 tablespoons margarine

¾ cup pecans
1 teaspoon vanilla
1½ tablespoons marshmallow
  creme (optional)

Mix sugar, milk, and corn syrup in a heavy saucepan. Cook to soft ball stage, 230 degrees. Remove from heat and stir in margarine, pecans, vanilla, and marshmallow creme. Let cool until mixture begins to thicken at bottom, then beat until it becomes light in color.

Drop by spoonfuls onto buttered wax paper. Let them spread out and "set" before serving.

Yield: 2 dozen
Special Equipment: Candy thermometer

Rum Truffles

. . . .

3 ounces semi-sweet chocolate

1 egg yolk

1 tablespoon butter

1 tablespoon dark rum

1 teaspoon heavy cream

2 ounces chocolate sprinkles

Melt chocolate in double boiler or in a bowl over pan of hot water. Add egg yolk, butter, rum, and cream. Beat mixture until thick. Chill one hour or until firm enough to handle.

Shape into small bite size balls and roll in sprinkles to cover. Store on wax paper in cool place.

Yield: 18 to 20 pieces
Special Equipment: Double boiler

Chocolate Peanut Butter Balls

. . . .

3 cups creamy peanut butter

2 pounds confectioners sugar

3 sticks butter, melted

2 cups (12 ounces) chocolate chips

4 ounces German Sweet chocolate

1 square paraffin wax

Mix peanut butter, sugar, and butter thoroughly. Form into balls and freeze.

Melt chocolate chips, German chocolate, and wax in double boiler. Dip frozen balls in chocolate. Keep refrigerated until serving.

Yield: 8 dozen
Special Equipment: Double boiler

Kids and grown-ups love these!

. . . .

White Chocolate Mousse

6 eggs, separated	9 ounces white chocolate
Dash of salt	½ cup sweet butter
3 tablespoons rum	1¾ cups heavy cream, whipped
1 teaspoon vanilla	to soft peaks
½ cup plus 1 tablespoon	
granulated sugar	

Over medium heat in top of double boiler, beat egg yolks, salt, rum, vanilla, and sugar until thick, then remove top of double boiler from heat and let cool.

In second pot, melt chocolate over lightly simmering water. When chocolate is completely melted, beat in butter. Remove from heat.

Gradually beat egg yolk mixture into chocolate mixture. After mixing, slowly whisk in whipped cream. Pour into fancy bowl or 1 quart souffle dish with collar of wax paper or foil. Freeze.

Take out early in the day to serve for dinner. After mousse defrosts, refrigerate until needed.

Serves: 6

Special Equipment: Double boiler

Lime Mousse

5 eggs	2 cups heavy cream
1 cup sugar	1 tablespoon freshly grated lime
1 stick sweet butter, melted and cooled	zest (4 to 5 limes)
1 cup fresh lime juice (6 to 8 limes)	Fresh raspberries for garnish (optional)

In large bowl combine eggs and sugar. Beat at medium speed until pale, about 5 minutes. Beat in melted butter in a thin stream. Add lime juice.

Pour mixture into top of double boiler. Cook over moderate heat, whisking constantly, until mixture thickens, about 15 minutes.

Transfer custard to medium bowl and refrigerate for at least 1 hour, stirring once or twice.

In large bowl, beat heavy cream until it forms soft peaks. Fold cream into chilled custard. Fold in lime zest. Serve in chilled stem glasses, garnish with fresh raspberries.

Serves: 6 to 8

Special Equipment: Double boiler

Pots de Crème Grand Marnier

2 cups heavy cream
4 egg yolks
5 tablespoons granulated sugar
⅛ teaspoon salt

1 tablespoon grated orange rind
2 tablespoons Grand Marnier
Orange rind to garnish

Place cream in saucepan and bring almost to a boil.

Beat egg yolks, sugar, and salt together until light and lemon colored. Gradually add heated cream to egg yolks, stirring with wire whisk.

Place saucepan over low heat or use double boiler and stir with a wooden spoon until custard thickens and coats spoon. Set saucepan in basin of cold water to stop cooking.

Stir in grated orange rind and Grand Marnier. Pour into individual custard cups and chill thoroughly. Garnish with orange rind.

Serves: 6 to 8
Special Equipment: Double boiler (optional)/Custard cups

Molded French Cream

. . . .

1 cup sour cream	8 ounces cream cheese, room temperature
1 cup heavy cream	½ teaspoon vanilla
¾ cup extra fine granulated sugar	1 pint fresh strawberries; or seasonal fruit
1 envelope unflavored gelatin	
¼ cup water	

Brush 4 cup mold lightly with vegetable oil.

Combine sour cream and heavy cream in medium saucepan. Beat in sugar. Place over low heat to warm while preparing gelatin.

Sprinkle gelatin over water in cup to soften. Place cup in pan of hot water to dissolve. Stir gelatin into warm cream mixture and remove from heat.

Beat cream cheese with electric mixer until soft. Add to warm cream mixture gradually. Add vanilla and blend thoroughly. Pour into prepared mold. Refrigerate overnight.

When ready to serve dip mold into hot water for 10 seconds. Unmold onto serving plate. Surround with fresh strawberries or fruit in season.

Serves: 10
Special Equipment: 4 cup mold

. . . .

Bananas Flambé

4 small bananas
4 tablespoons butter
¼ cup sugar

¼ cup dark rum
1 teaspoon vanilla

Peel bananas and cut in half lengthwise.

In large frying pan, melt butter over medium heat. Stir in sugar. Add bananas. Cook, turning frequently until lightly browned and tender, about 5 minutes. Remove from heat.

In a small saucepan, warm rum and vanilla over low heat. Ignite with a match and pour over bananas. Serve immediately.

Serves: 4

Rhubarb Delight

3 cups sliced rhubarb
2 cups water
⅓ cup minute tapioca
Pinch salt

1 cup sugar
1 orange, juice and rind
Vanilla ice cream or whipped cream

Bring rhubarb to boil in water. Reduce heat, add tapioca, salt, sugar, orange juice, and rind. Stir until sugar dissolves. Cook over low heat until rhubarb is soft. Chill. Top with whipped cream or serve over vanilla ice cream.

Serves: 8 to 10

Heavenly Peach Dessert

⅓ cup butter
1½ teaspoons cinnamon
3 fresh peaches, peeled and
  halved

½ cup honey
Vanilla ice cream
½ cup fresh or frozen raspberries

Melt butter in a medium frying pan. Stir in cinnamon. Add peach halves; cook until heated through, about 5 minutes.

Gently stir in honey. Simmer uncovered, stirring and basting occasionally until sauce is thickened, about 8 minutes.

Scoop ice cream into 6 dessert dishes. Place a peach half on the ice cream, cut-side down. Spoon warm honey sauce over top. Garnish with whole raspberries.

Serves: 6

This is elegant served in heavy wine goblets.

Caramelized Oranges

12 medium-sized navel oranges
1 cup sugar
1¼ cups water

4 to 5 tablespoons rum
Cherries
Fresh mint leaves

Remove peel and pith from oranges. Set oranges aside to be used later.

Slice half the peel into thin strips. Reserve rest of peel for garnish.

Add sliced peel to half of water. Soak for one hour. Cover and simmer over very low flame for 20 minutes. Set aside.

Combine remaining 5 ounces of water and sugar in heavy saucepan. Stir over low heat until sugar dissolves. Boil steadily without stirring until sugar begins to brown and carmelize.

Strain liquid from orange peel into caramel. Stir over low heat until blended; add rum. Dribble sauce over reserved oranges. Garnish with uncooked orange peels, decoratively sliced. Chill. May also garnish with cherries or fresh mint leaves.

Serves: 12

Strawberries and Blueberries Sabayon

4 egg yolks

⅓ cup sugar

¾ cup cream sherry

1 quart strawberries

1 pint blueberries

1 cup toasted almonds (or 1 cup shaved chocolate)

In top of double boiler, whisk egg yolks, sugar, and sherry, simmering until thick and creamy. Clean fruit. Slice strawberries. Pour sauce over fruit, garnish with almonds or shaved chocolate.

Serves: 8
Special Equipment: Double boiler

Yogurt and Cream Cheese Confection

8 ounces cream cheese, softened

8 ounces orange or raspberry yogurt

¼ cup coconut

1 teaspoon orange rind, grated

1 tablespoon honey

Combine all ingredients. Refrigerate 2 hours. Serve over sliced fruit for breakfast or as a dessert.

Serves: 8 to 10

Caramel Sauce

1 14-ounce can sweetened
  condensed milk
¾ cup light corn syrup
½ cup sugar
⅓ cup brown sugar, firmly
  packed

¼ cup butter or margarine
¼ cup whipping cream
1½ teaspoons vanilla extract
Ice cream or pound cake

Combine first 4 ingredients in heavy saucepan and mix well. Cook over medium heat, stirring constantly, until mixture reaches 220 degrees on candy thermometer. Remove from heat. Stir in butter, whipping cream, and vanilla. Serve warm over ice cream or pound cake.

Yield: 3 Cups
Special Equipment: Candy thermometer

Serve over Pound Cake on page 221.

Clambake on Jones Beach

Restaurant
Recipes

"Tips From The Pros"

An island of eight million people requires a substantial variety of diversions. Museums, historic restorations, botanical gardens, and famous "Gold Coast" mansions attract visitors, while orchestras, dance companies and theater groups provide entertainment throughout the year.

A sample of Island museums includes the Brooklyn, Heckscher, Nassau County and Parrish museums of fine arts, the Children's Museum in Brooklyn, the Black History Museum in Hempstead, the Queens Museum (containing a diorama of New York City), Sag Harbor and Cold Spring Harbor whaling museums, and the innovative Museum of the Moving Image in Queens.

The Museums at Stony Brook, Garvies Point Museum, the Cold Spring Harbor Fish Hatchery, Planting Fields and Bayard Cutting Arboretums, and Old Bethpage Village Restoration are just a few of the other cultural attractions available to visitors.

Both residents and newcomers appreciate Long Island for its educational as well as recreational opportunities. Thirty-two colleges and universities in the four counties challenge thousands of scholars each year. They include the U.S. Merchant Marine Academy at Kings Point, Hofstra, Adelphi, and St. John's universities and several branches of New York State University.

Our proximity to New York City enhances the opportunity to attract top-rank entertainers and musicians to our stages. The Long Island Philharmonic, Tilles Center for the Performing Arts, and the Long Island Youth Orchestra, among others, give classical music lovers a host of choices while Jones Beach Theater, Westbury Music Fair, and Nassau Coliseum regularly feature popular entertainment.

Baked Scallops in Pesto

2 pounds scallops
¼ cup white wine
2 tablespoons lemon juice,
    freshly squeezed
2 cups fresh basil

¾ cup Parmesan cheese
3 cloves garlic, peeled
¼ cup pine nuts, toasted
½ cup olive oil

Mix wine and lemon juice and pour over scallops. Set aside.

In food processor combine basil, cheese, garlic, pine nuts, and olive oil.

Add basil mixture to scallops, stirring until scallops are well coated.

Place in 6-quart casserole dish. Bake at 425 degrees for 10 to 15 minutes.

Serves: 4 to 6
Special Equipment: Food Processor

Restaurant: **The Barge at Capri**
                86 Orchard Beach Boulevard
                Port Washington

Oysters Chardonnay

24 artichoke hearts, canned

24 oysters, canned or fresh

2 ounces butter

1 pound fresh spinach, well
washed and chopped

4 ounces onion, minced

2 ounces garlic, peeled and
minced

¼ cup Pernod

Salt and pepper to taste

Mornay Sauce:

1½ pints heavy cream

2 ounces flour

2 ounces butter

Salt and pepper to taste

1 cup Swiss cheese, grated

½ cup Parmesan cheese, freshly
grated

2 egg yolks

Hollow out center leaves of artichoke hearts and trim bottoms so they will stand up without tipping over.

Shuck oysters (if fresh), and place into the hollowed-out artichoke hearts. In a saucepan, heat the butter and sauté spinach. Add onion, garlic, salt and pepper. Stir and add Pernod. Put aside to cool. While this mixture is cooling, make Mornay Sauce.

Heat heavy cream in saucepan.

Melt butter in another pan, whisk in flour and cook approximately 5 minutes, stirring so it will not burn.

Continued on next page

Add heated heavy cream to flour and butter mixture (roux), whisking it in a little at a time until medium to thick sauce results. Season to taste.

Add cheeses and stir until they are melted and incorporated into sauce. Remove from heat.

Lightly beat egg yolks. Add ½ cup sauce to eggs and stir. Return egg yolk mixture to sauce, whisking it in slowly.

When spinach mixture is cool, stir in ¾ cup of Mornay sauce. Place ½ to 1 tablespoon spinach mixture on stuffed hearts.

Place hearts on 1-inch deep cookie sheet with ¼ inch of water on bottom. Bake at 375 degrees for about 10 minutes or until hot.

Ladle Mornay sauce over each stuffed artichoke heart and place under broiler until sauce turns golden brown. Serve 4 to each guest.

Serves: 6

Restaurant: **Chardonnay's Restaurant**
Long Island Marriott
101 James Doolittle Boulevard
Uniondale

Vegetarian Chili

⅓ cup olive oil

2 cups onion, chopped

¾ cup celery, chopped

1 cup green pepper, chopped

1 cup carrots, chopped

1 tablespoon garlic, minced

2 cups fresh mushrooms, quartered

¼ teaspoon red pepper flakes

1 tablespoon ground cumin

¾ teaspoon basil

2 to 4 tablespoons chili powder

¾ teaspoon oregano

2 teaspoons salt (optional)

½ teaspoon pepper

2 cups tomato juice

¾ cup barley

2 cups fresh tomatoes, chopped

2 cups kidney beans with juice

Tabasco sauce to taste

2 tablespoons lemon juice

3 tablespoons tomato paste

1 tablespoon Worcestershire sauce

¼ cup red wine

2 tablespoons green chili peppers, chopped

Heat olive oil in large enameled pot. Add chopped vegetables and sauté 4 to 5 minutes.

Add garlic, pepper flakes, cumin, basil, chili powder, oregano, and salt and sauté another minute.

Add remaining ingredients and simmer for 25 minutes, uncovered.

Restaurant: **Culinary Heights, Inc.**
174 7th Street
Garden City

Poppy Seed Dressing

1 egg
½ cup onion, diced
¼ cup Dijon mustard
½ cup poppy seeds

¼ cup sugar
1 cup champagne vinegar
3 cups corn oil

Crack egg in bowl. Add onion, mustard, poppy seeds, sugar, and vinegar. Slowly whip in oil to form thick dressing.

Keep refrigerated.

May be used on green leaf salads or any cooked, fresh chilled vegetables or fruits.

Yield: 4 cups

Restaurant: **The Culinary Studio Gourmet Food Shoppe**
136 Wall Street
Huntington

Fresh Spinach Salad with Bay Shrimp and Honey Mustard Dressing

Salad:

1 pound fresh spinach, stems removed, well washed and dried

6 slices crisp bacon, diced

1 hard-cooked egg, chopped

4 ounces cooked shrimp, peeled, deveined, and sliced lengthwise

4 cherry tomatoes

Dressing:

1 raw egg yolk

1 ounce red wine vinegar

1 ounce honey

¼ teaspoon garlic, minced

1 tablespoon Dijon mustard

½ ounce bacon fat

3 ounces soybean oil

Salt and pepper to taste

Place egg yolk in stainless-steel bowl with vinegar, honey, garlic, and mustard. Mix with wire whisk. Combine bacon fat and oil and slowly add to egg yolk mixture, stirring until all ingredients are blended thoroughly.

Place dry spinach on salad plate and sprinkle bacon and chopped egg over spinach. Arrange shrimp and cherry tomatoes on egg and bacon. Drizzle dressing over salad and serve.

Serves: 4 to 6

Restaurant: **Danford's Inn at Bayles Dock**
East Broadway
Port Jefferson

Piccata Al Limone

8 ounces veal scallopini
Flour
2 tablespoons soybean oil
¼ pound butter

1 cup white wine
Salt and pepper to taste
¼ cup fresh parsley, chopped
½ fresh lemon

Cut veal into four slices and pound until thin. Dredge in flour and sauté in hot oil until juices from veal are no longer pink. Remove veal to a warmed platter.

Discard oil and add butter, wine, salt, pepper, and parsley to sauté pan. Cook over medium-high heat until sauce is reduced and thickened. Add lemon juice. Pour sauce over veal and serve immediately.

Serves: 4

Restaurant: **DiMaggio's Restaurant & Pizzeria**
706 Port Washington Boulevard
Port Washington

Baked Monkfish with Sauerkraut and Caraway

8 10-ounce portions of monkfish
   filets

8 ounces brown stock of veal
   (substitute beef broth)

2 ounces prepared tomato sauce

1 teaspoon whole caraway seed

2 ounces shallots, minced

1 ounce sugar

2 ounces margarine

2 ounces butter

Salt and pepper to taste

1 cup prepared sauerkraut,
   drained

Marinade:

1 pint vegetable oil

1 ounce onion, chopped

1 clove garlic, peeled and
   crushed

1 teaspoon whole caraway seed

Salt and pepper to taste

Marinate monkfish for 24 hours. Remove and pat dry when ready for cooking.

In a 7-inch saucepan place margarine, butter, and sugar. Carmelize over low heat. Add shallots and caraway. Increase heat and add fish, searing the filet.

Remove fish and lower heat. Add sauerkraut, stir, and add stock and tomato sauce. Return fish to pan and place over sauerkraut. Put pan into 500 degree oven and bake approximately 15 to 20 minutes or until fish is done.

Continued on next page

Continued Baked Monkfish with Sauerkraut and Caraway

When fish is ready, remove from pan, place pan over high heat and reduce sauerkraut and sauce until almost dry. Season to taste.

On a hot charcoal grill mark the monkfish as you would a cut of meat or sausage. Place on top of sauerkraut.

Accompany with roasted potatoes and a compote of apple cranberry garnish and serve hot.

Serves: 8
Special Equipment: Grill

Winner of New York State Seafood Challenge 1988.

Restaurant: **Deep Sea Dive**
181 Main Street
Port Washington

Chicken Victory

1 pound boneless chicken
  breasts, skinned

½ cup flour

¼ cup vegetable oil

1 teaspoon shallot, finely
  chopped

½ cup fresh mushrooms, sliced

½ cup diced tomatoes

¼ cup white wine

2 tablespoons Dijon mustard

½ cup heavy cream

¼ cup chicken stock

Salt and pepper to taste

2 tablespoons scallions, sliced

Dredge chicken in flour. Shake off excess.

In sauté pan heat oil and sauté chicken lightly on both sides. Remove chicken and drain oil from pan.

Return chicken and add shallots, mushrooms, and tomatoes and cook together for 15 seconds. Add white wine and cook over very low heat.

In a separate bowl mix mustard and cream together and add to chicken. Pour in chicken stock and simmer for 6 to 8 minutes.

Season to taste. Garnish with scallions before serving.

Serves: 4

Restaurant: **George Washington Manor**
               1305 Old Northern Boulevard
               Roslyn

Red Snapper with Orange Sauce and Cashews

4 8 to 10-ounce red snapper
filets, skinned and boned

Flour, seasoned with salt and
pepper

2 ounces butter

1 cup roasted cashews

1 orange, halved

Salt and pepper to taste

Fresh parsley, chopped

Put 1 ounce butter in sauté pan large enough to hold four filets. Heat until butter begins to brown.

While butter is melting, dust fish with flour and place in hot pan. Let brown about 2 minutes on each side.

Remove fish to a warmed platter and drain butter. Add remaining butter and cashews to pan and cook until golden brown.

Season to taste and add parsley. Finish by squeezing the juice of one orange into the pan. Spoon sauce over fish.

Garnish with fresh orange slices or wedges and sprigs of fresh parsley or mint.

Serves: 4

Restaurant: **La Pace**
50 Cedar Swamp Road
Glen Cove

Swiss Bisque with Ham

1 cup bacon drippings
1 cup flour
2 quarts chicken stock, heated

1 quart heavy cream
2 pounds ham, chopped
3 pounds Swiss cheese, grated

Heat bacon drippings and add flour. Cook over medium heat, stirring well for about 2 minutes. Be careful not to burn.

Slowly add heated stock, stirring constantly with wire whisk.

When thickened, lower heat and simmer for about 30 minutes. Add ham and cream. Simmer an additional 20 minutes.

Whisk in cheese. Serve immediately.

Serves: 12

Restaurant: **Latitudes**
Orchard Beach Boulevard
Port Washington

Pâtés Fraiches Au Saumon Fumé

1 tablespoon shallots, finely chopped
¼ cup chicken stock
½ cup heavy cream
4 servings fresh pasta
1 tablespoon olive oil
8 ounces smoked salmon

¼ cup white wine
2 teaspoons tomato paste
½ stick sweet butter
4 tablespoons fresh Parmesan cheese, grated
1 tablespoon chives, chopped
Salt and pepper

In a casserole, reduce the white wine and chicken stock with the chopped shallots.

When liquid is almost evaporated, add the tomato paste and the cream, stir well with a whisk, and reduce to two-thirds. Remove from heat and incorporate the butter a tablespoon at a time with the whisk. Add salt and pepper to taste.

Cook the pasta in rapidly boiling water until al dente and drain well. Add one tablespoon of olive oil, salt and pepper, and mix well.

Drain the sauce through a strainer into the bottom of four plates. Place pasta on the sauce. Sprinkle 1 tablespoon of cheese and 2 ounces of salmon over each serving. Garnish with chives. Serve immediately.

Serves: 4

Restaurant: Mirabelle
404 North Country Road
St. James

Pasta Primavera

1 head broccoli florets
1 head cauliflower florets
4 carrots, julienned
1 small box frozen peas
6 cloves garlic, peeled and
   crushed

1½ cups olive oil
3½ cups chicken broth
2 pounds vermicelli

Blanch vegetables except peas. Run under cold water to maintain color after blanching.

Run hot water over frozen peas.

Heat oil. Add crushed garlic and sauté until it turns slightly brown. Add boiling broth (carefully) to hot oil and simmer for 15 minutes.

Cook pasta until al dente.

Pour garlic/oil sauce over pasta. Add vegetables and toss. Serve at room temperature.

Serves: 8 to 10

Restaurant: **Munday's**
                259 Main Street
                Huntington

Grilled Chicken Dijonaise

1 3-pound chicken, halved
1 teaspoon thyme
1 tablespoon tarragon
1 small onion, finely chopped

8 ounces Dijon mustard
5 ounces olive oil
2 ounces water

Combine all ingredients except chicken. Pour mixture over chicken and marinate in refrigerator for 24 hours.

Bake at 450 degrees for 20 minutes or until flesh is white, or place on grill or hot barbecue for 20 minutes.

Serves: 4 To 6
Special Equipment: Barbecue grill

Restaurant: **Panama Hatties**
872 East Jericho Turnpike
Huntington Station

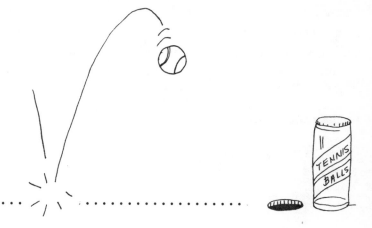

Pasta Del Mese Di Maggio

⅓ cup olive oil
3 ounces butter
1 ounce prosciutto ham, diced
Pinch black pepper
4 or 5 medium asparagus spears
3 cups frozen artichoke hearts
3 cups broccoli florets
2 cups frozen peas

½ cup chicken stock
½ ounce salt
½ pound white fettuccine
½ pound green fettuccine
6 ounces pesto sauce (pre-made)
3 ounces Parmesan cheese, freshly grated

In a large skillet heat butter, olive oil, prosciutto, and pepper.

When prosciutto gets brown add asparagus, artichokes, broccoli, and peas, stirring each for 1 minute before adding the next.

Add chicken stock and continue to stir for 30 seconds to 1 minute. Turn off heat. Push all vegetables to sides of the pan, creating an opening in center.

In separate pot bring 3 quarts water to boil. Add ½ ounce salt, then fettuccini. Cook 3 to 4 minutes if using fresh pasta, or 10 to 12 minutes if using boxed pasta. When pasta is cooked, drain well and pour into center of skillet. Turn heat under skillet back on to low.

Using 2 forks, start lifting and mixing pasta into vegetables. Add pesto sauce and two-thirds of cheese. Continue to sauté 1 more minute. Turn onto serving platter, sprinkle with remaining cheese, and serve.

Serves: 6 to 8

Restaurant: Razzano's
80 Main Street
Port Washington

Swordfish Grenoblaise

4 10-ounce swordfish steaks
Flour
2 ounces cooking oil
2 tablespoons butter
2 or 3 shallots, chopped

2 teaspoons Dijon mustard
1 teaspoon capers
6 ounces white wine
1 pint heavy cream

Dredge swordfish in flour and brown in hot oil. Remove fish from pan and keep warm.

Drain oil and add butter. Sauté shallots until tender. Add mustard, capers, wine, and cream. Cook over medium heat for approximately 6 minutes or until sauce has reduced and thickened.

Spoon over swordfish and serve immediately.

Serves: 4

Restaurant: **Tee T's Landing**
95 New York Avenue
Halesite

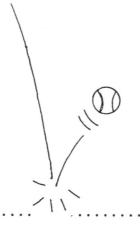

Cold Plum Soup

1 large (1 pound, 13 ounce) can
   purple plums

1 cup water

⅔ cup sugar

1 cinnamon stick

¼ teaspoon white pepper

Pinch salt

½ cup heavy cream

½ cup dry red wine

1 tablespoon cornstarch

2 tablespoons fresh lemon juice

1 teaspoon lemon rind, grated

1 cup sour cream

3 tablespoons brandy

Drain plums, reserving syrup, and pit and chop the plums.

In a saucepan, combine the plums with the reserved syrup, water, sugar, cinnamon stick, white pepper, and salt and bring to a boil over moderately high heat.

Stir in heavy cream and red wine mixed with cornstarch and cook the mixture, stirring until thickened. Stir in lemon juice and lemon rind and remove pan from the heat.

In a small bowl, whisk sour cream into ½ cup of the soup and add brandy. Stir the mixture into the soup until smooth. Let the soup cool and then refrigerate it, covered, for at least 4 hours.

Ladle the soup into cups and garnish each serving with a dollop of sour cream and a sprinkling of cinnamon.

Serves: 6 to 8

Restaurant: Three Village Inn
                150 Main Street
                Stony Brook

Chicken Scarpariello

3 pounds chicken cutlets, cut into 14 pieces

4 ounces olive oil

2 teaspoons garlic, minced

1 teaspoon Italian parsley, finely chopped

Salt, pepper and rosemary to taste

1 cup water

Wash chicken pieces in warm water and dry throughly. Put chicken into skillet with very hot oil. Cook until chicken is nicely browned on all sides.

Discard all but 2 tablespoons of the oil, add the garlic, and sauté with chicken until the garlic is golden brown. Add parsley, salt, pepper, and rosemary. Stir briefly and add water. Cover the pan and let cook on low heat for 10 to 15 minutes.

Serves: 6

Restaurant: **Trattoria DeMeo**
1051 Northern Boulevard
Roslyn

Penne with Shrimp and Asparagus Tips

. . . .

1 pound penne pasta

8 large shrimp, peeled, deveined, and cooked

12 asparagus tips, steamed for 12 minutes and cut in bite-size pieces

4 ounces fresh tomato sauce

1 pint heavy cream

2 tablespoons butter

2 ounces white wine

1 clove garlic, peeled and minced

Fresh parsley, finely chopped

Salt and pepper to taste

Cook penne in 4 quarts of salted boiling water until al dente.

While pasta is cooking, sauté garlic in butter in a large skillet. Add shrimp and asparagus to the garlic. Stir in tomato sauce and wine. Simmer for 2 minutes. Add heavy cream and salt and pepper.

Drain penne very well and combine with shrimp sauce over low heat until pasta is well coated. Sprinkle with parsley.

Serves: 4 to 6

Restaurant: **Villa Gattapardo**
Old Northern Boulevard
Roslyn

Crème Brulée

. . . .

½ cup dark brown sugar
3 cups heavy cream
1 vanilla bean, split
6 egg yolks

¾ cup granulated sugar
Pinch of salt
3 teaspoons brown sugar

Spread brown sugar in thin layer in cake pan. Dry sugar near pilot light in oven for 24 hours, or set aside at room temperature for 48 hours. Rake sugar frequently with fingers. Adjust oven rack to lowest position. Heat oven to 300 degrees.

Combine cream and vanilla bean in large saucepan; heat until warm.

In a large bowl, mix egg yolks with salt and sugar. Gradually whisk in cream. Strain through a double-mesh sieve into 6 ungreased ½-cup ramekins.

Transfer ramekins to a jelly roll pan. Pour hot water into pan to come halfway up the outside of the ramekins. Bake for 20 to 45 minutes, or until custard is just set. If bubbles appear on surface, custard will be overcooked. Let cool, then refrigerate.

At serving time, sprinkle ½ teaspoon unbaked brown sugar in a thin layer over each ramekin. Place custard under broiler, close to heat source, until sugar caramelizes. Serve immediately.

Serves: 6
Special Equipment: Double-mesh sieve/6 ½-cup ramekins

Restaurant: Zanghi's
50 Forest Avenue
Glen Cove

. . . .

Index

Order Additional Copies

··

IT'S OUR SERVE!
1395 Old Northern Blvd., Roslyn, N.Y. 11576   (516) 484-0649

Please send me ___ copies of IT'S OUR SERVE! $16.95 each
Postage and handling $ 2.50 each
*Gift wrap (optional) $ 1.00 each

                              Total Enclosed _____

Name _____

Address _____

City _____ State _____ Zip _____
    ☐ Check or money order enclosed
    ☐ Visa/Mastercard No. _____ Exp. date _____
    Signature _____ Interbank No. _____

* If shipping to multiple addresses, or gift card needed, please attach.

All proceeds from IT'S OUR SERVE! support projects of the Junior League of Long Island, a non-profit, volunteer organization committed to improving the quality of life in our community.

··

IT'S OUR SERVE!
1395 Old Northern Blvd., Roslyn, N.Y. 11576   (516) 484-0649

Please send me ___ copies of IT'S OUR SERVE! $16.95 each
Postage and handling $ 2.50 each
*Gift wrap (optional) $ 1.00 each

                              Total Enclosed _____

Name _____

Address _____

City _____ State _____ Zip _____
    ☐ Check or money order enclosed
    ☐ Visa/Mastercard No. _____ Exp. date _____
    Signature _____ Interbank No. _____

* If shipping to multiple addresses, or gift card needed, please attach.

All proceeds from IT'S OUR SERVE! support projects of the Junior League of Long Island, a non-profit, volunteer organization committed to improving the quality of life in our community.

··

I would like the following individuals to receive information on IT'S OUR SERVE!

Name _____   Name _____

Address _____   Address _____

City _____   City _____

State ____ Zip _____   State ____ Zip _____

I would like to see IT'S OUR SERVE! in the following stores in my area.

Store Name _____   Store Name _____

Address _____   Address _____

City _____   City _____

State ____ Zip _____   State ____ Zip _____

I would like the following individuals to receive information on IT'S OUR SERVE!

Name _____   Name _____

Address _____   Address _____

City _____   City _____

State ____ Zip _____   State ____ Zip _____

I would like to see IT'S OUR SERVE! in the following stores in my area.

Store Name _____   Store Name _____

Address _____   Address _____

City _____   City _____

State ____ Zip _____   State ____ Zip _____